T0301223

BAD INFLUENCE

BAD INFLUENCE

Reflections on a life lived online

INFLUENCE

OENONE FORBAT

QUERCUS

First published in Great Britain in 2023 by

QUERCUS

Quercus Editions Ltd
Carmelite House
50 Victoria Embankment
London EC4Y 0DZ

An Hachette UK company

A CIP catalogue record for this book is available
from the British Library

HB ISBN 978 1 52942 389 1
TPB ISBN 978 1 52942 390 7
Ebook ISBN 978 1 52942 393 8

Some names and identifying details have been changed to protect the privacy of individuals.

10 9 8 7 6 5 4 3 2

Typeset by Jouve (UK), Milton Keynes
Printed and bound in Great Britain by Clays Ltd, Elcograf S.p.A.

Papers used by Quercus are from well-managed forests and other responsible sources.

For my girls

Preface

'I REALLY HATE being called an influencer,' I sighed to my agent during a meandering phone call about my career after yet another identity crisis. She laughed and said, 'Write about it then.' So here we are.

I'm old enough to remember when 'influence' was a neutral word. You had to put an adjective in front of it to give it a moral dimension. When I was growing up, Emma Watson was often wheeled out by the media as a 'good influence', whereas your mum's favourite example of a 'bad influence' was someone who dared you and all your friends to jump off a bridge. Nowadays, social media influencers often get a bad rap. Spawned from the loins of the internet, they are seen as greedy, brain-dead reprobates with a penchant for gaudy designer clothes, scams and misinformation. And they *would*, most likely,

1

dare you and five of your closest friends to plummet to your death off the side of the Clifton Suspension Bridge, all while livestreaming it for their vlog with the message 'Merch to follow!' That isn't the sort of person I strive to be (although I am happy to – and have been known to – wear gaudy designer clothes).

I guess I ought to explain what an influencer is – what I am. The word 'influencer' means different things to different people. For some, it's the way they describe their favourite content creator, for others it's how they insult their least favourite reality star. The dictionary defines it as 'a person with the ability to influence potential buyers of a product or service by promoting or recommending the items on social media.' That's not incorrect, because being an influencer is, according to its most cynical definition, about making life as 'shoppable' as possible. Whether you need a haircut, new shoes, or cream for your haemorrhoids, there's an influencer out there for you. To sceptics, out of nowhere we light up your smartphone with a pack of slim-tummy tea in hand, our glossy hair tagged as a brand of vitamin gummies and our fingers crossed behind our back: Double-O Bimbo, licence to be ridiculed. But for some people, how easy it is to shop – via their favourite influencer's story swipe-up links, detailed newsletter or regularly updated highlights – is a godsend. It's like having a personalised version of your preferred fashion magazine, optimised with styles that suit your body shape, are within your budget and available to purchase in just a few steps.

With social media we can search for people whose lives we're interested in, inspired by or can otherwise relate to. Where magazines used to give us *their* opinions on who is 'best dressed', 'most eligible' or has the 'worst beach body' – all the while presenting us with a slew of lookalike models that all fit the script for, well, being a model – social media, despite all its foibles, gives us something new. It gives us perceived agency, more diversity and a feeling that the people we follow are, in a lot of ways, just like us.

So that's the money-making part, but there's a lot more to it than that. An influencer is a friend in your pocket and many people follow influencers not for their ads, outfits or discount codes, but for who they are as a person. That might seem a step away from the natural order of organic human interaction, but then every year millions of people report feeling lonely, so if this works as a plaster for the wound then maybe we shouldn't be so quick to judge? Between the carefully created flat lays, filtered adverts and posed photos, there are pockets of intimacy, vulnerability and humanity, and influencers having a positive impact on individuals and society at large. Often, people follow influencers in spite of the fact that we promote products on our pages. Many people just want to get to know us, be inspired by our style, ask our advice on relationships or what TV show to watch next, or simply be entertained.

As I'll explain later, the paradoxical tug of war at the centre of the influencer economy is that once you get good at growing and engaging an audience, in order to sustain a level of communication with your followers that will keep them engaged and fulfilled, it needs to be your full-time job. Very, very few people have the money, resources or hours it takes to be plugged in to their phone talking to people online all day. Once it starts to become that time-consuming, you either go all in or give up and stick to the day job. If you *can* monetise a social media platform, the life afforded to you by the profession may suddenly start to feel very unattainable. Brands start to gift you things, restaurants invite you to try their new menu, salons offer you free blow-dries. That isn't because those are things that ordinary people would or should do with such regularity, but because influencers are in a position to show their followers what they *could* do, buy or enjoy.

There are millions of places to eat, shop and be pampered in, but we try them out not just for fun (even if it is, sometimes), but because that's our job! However, that's when we are accused of misrepresenting the world to a captive audience, who then must come to terms with the fact that their own lives might be much less glamorous and unbridled than ours. And this is why it is complicated. The content that consumers want, can, for the most part, only exist in a world where creators have the time and resources to make it. It just so happens that the by-product of creating content that brings in followers is an extremely lucrative advertising space. Influencers act as the menu, displaying your options, but unlike the models in the pages of magazines who are paid by the hour to be a clothes horse for items they can't keep, we get to experience and keep a myriad of products and experiences. That being said, no one would gift me a Dyson Airwrap if there wasn't the possibility that you might buy one because of me. I am not special, it is you, my audience, that brands really want. Influencers create a path of almost no resistance for brands to reach consumers and that, well, that's worth a lot.

It can seem as though influencers were immaculately conceived in the wet dreams of Kevin Systrom, Jack Dorsey and Mark Zuckerberg. But just like Frankenstein, are we the monsters they created or are they the monsters for creating us? Or perhaps we aren't monsters at all. In Sarah Frier's forensic examination of Instagram, *No Filter*, she speaks of how the founders were aware, even in the start-up stages, of harnessing the power of influential individuals in order to recruit more users. Even though influencers now manage their own ecosystems, the larger truth is that we all just drive more traffic to these platforms and their billionaire owners. In the early stages, the Instagram founders reached out to professionals who could take stunning, aspirational photographs, in order to encourage prospective users to download the app. They reasoned that others might sign up in the hopes that maybe they, too, could achieve the same, picture-perfect effect.

Whilst this was an early iteration of what we now understand influencers to be, it leads me to realise that my career path wasn't as accidental as it felt. I might've fallen into it, but the pit was dug intentionally, ready and waiting, and although the Instagram founders were initially against users profiting from their platform, that's exactly how I and tens of thousands of others now make our bread and butter: by advertising products to our followers. But even if they now encourage influencers, even creating tools to facilitate and monitor our work, my next pay cheque is still dependent on their whims. The algorithms and models under which we, creators and users alike, operate are designed by the gods of Silicon Valley. As such, we influencers are still mere mortals, cogs in a new system, but cogs nonetheless. Sometimes I think people forget that. The push and pull of the mechanics that make the platforms work influences us influencers as much as we influence you. It is changing, but truth be told the industry is still a little like the Wild West.

People are always desperate to peel back the curtain to see what goes on behind the 'tiles' of the Gram, but few really grasp how the industry works. I became an influencer before we were even called influencers. It was the first time in my life I could lay claim to getting somewhere before the mainstream. I am not into indie music. I can't say I really get behind music without words, like techno for example, or 'oontz oontz' music, as one Twitter user called it. Unless it's classical, of course, and by classical I mean the theme tunes to *Harry Potter* or *The Lord of the Rings*. I still listen to Corinne Bailey Rae, Jack Johnson and Norah Jones on rotation. My Spotify Wrapped is almost identical each year. I am not edgy, either. Even with multiple tattoos and piercings, I am more likely to be mistaken for a younger Geri Halliwell than Miley Cyrus. Such is the burden of my natural affliction: being basic.

It seems important to point out that 'basic' in relation to me could easily be interchanged with 'privileged'. I am the default white, blonde, blue-eyed, 'well-spoken' woman who has elbowed her way into the media for years and, in the grand scheme of things, elbowing is a very tame sport. Much like leaning in, nowadays, the effort middle-class, white, cis-women must exert in order to break the glass ceiling, really isn't worth writing a book about. Ground-breaking, I am not, but in 2015 I happened to be loitering about in just the right part of the internet at just the right time (with just the right privileges) to garner a not insubstantial number of followers. Maybe you were one of them? If you were, thank you! I literally wouldn't be sitting here right now, tapping away with my silly little acrylic nails, had it not been for you *googly-eyed tongue-sticking-out emoji*. Whilst I never saw myself as a trendsetter, once you have enough numbers at the top of your social media page, for better or for worse, everyone appoints you as one.

There's a derision that often lingers over the think pieces, articles and books written about us, and whilst often that attitude is not without merit, there are two sides to every story. I have spent most of my adult life online, so much so that it can be hard to extricate which parts of me are the 'real' me and which parts I have subconsciously edited, finetuned and maybe even exaggerated to suit being so hyper-visible. Perhaps, now, after all this time, they are one and the same. When it comes to influencers, social media and our internet use at large, it is a totally multifaceted, complex and a somewhat undefinable entity. An industry born from recognising the power of the 'girl next door' over traditional celebrity, that unintentionally birthed a whole new species of fame, power and was – across the board – game-changing.

Nevertheless, I will do my best to define, and maybe even endear you to, the secret life of influencers by weaving in my personal experiences – not all of them flattering. Being an influencer is one of the most gossiped about, lucrative and (of course) influential careers available; one that isn't even considered a 'real job' by many. This is the story of how I came to be one. Love us or loathe us, it doesn't look like this industry is going anywhere soon and, by the way, it's a fascinating world.

It was Christmas 2014, when I was twenty years old, that I propositioned my parents for money towards a personal trainer (henceforth PT). I was in the market for a 'revenge bod', but with the tight budget of a university student who splashed out on

Marlboro Golds (rather than sensibly learning how to roll, like everyone else), I couldn't afford to back this project on my own. This financial illiteracy on my part meant that, despite working my way through university at various retail stores, night clubs and restaurants, I couldn't stretch my income to cover the costs and had to seek a contribution from my parents. They eventually, begrudgingly, generously, acquiesced to the couple hundred pounds I needed to secure my place with a well-known PT in the Cardiff area as a Christmas present. This would turn out to be the initial investment in my long-term career. I had found him via social media, of course, and his success was growing rapidly, almost entirely due to his client transformation photos. I signed up for a six-week course which took me from a slim size ten to a tiny, very lean and wholly unsustainable (for me) size six.

Little did I know back then that a cash injection from the proverbial bank of mum and dad, an eye-wateringly low body fat percentage and the sharing of my dramatic weight loss by my social media-savvy PT was the starter pack I needed to become a published author. I have wanted to be a writer ever since I read my first book, but never actually thought it was something I would be able to pursue. I spent most of my childhood either reading, writing or daydreaming stories. I am a storyteller by nature and by that I mean it's hard to get a word in edgeways around me, although I am working on it.

I have a flair for being dramatic and my friends will tell you that I never let facts get in the way of a good story, even if it means them sitting tight-lipped, smiling knowingly at each other, as I embellish our anecdotes with extra flavour, shall we say. For a long while I wanted to be a spy. I diligently watched *Harriet the Spy* on repeat from the age of five to around fifteen. We had it on rotation on VHS, along with *Free Willy*, *Fly Away Home*, and *The Witches* (I also tried to be a witch for much longer than I care to admit). I used to surreptitiously hide away in my room at uni doing the MI6 aptitude tests, secretly hoping that maybe, one day, I could become an agent. And then I went on to work in one of the most conspicuous industries ever conceived. But, against all odds, this strange career path of mine has landed me here, writing this book, so as much as I want to distance myself from the fitness industry with the swiftness in which I (almost accidentally) found myself in it, this is a shoutout to my abs!

Chapter 1

In july 2013, after sixth form, I took a gap year. If you've ever heard me speak, this probably won't come as much of a surprise. Only a couple of years prior, the now infamous *Gap Yah* video had gone viral on You-Tube. It was a hilariously quotable satire of privately educated British students like me and every time I told anyone I was going to Ecuador, they responded with 'On your gap yaaah? Are you gonna vomcano?'

I persisted. I wanted to get away from everything I'd always known and learn a thing or two (or three) about myself. I spent six weeks teaching indigenous children Spanish (which again, feels very ripe for parody) before I came home to work in a Jack Wills outlet (this is not a Josh Berry skit – this is all true). By living at home and selling discounted stripey knickers, pheasant-adorned notebooks and preppy gilets (a friend of mine recently referred to these as 'Chelsea life jackets'), I saved enough money to fly to Thailand on a group trip with one of my school friends. After this soft version of mind-expanding travel, which primarily consisted of drinking from coconuts on the beach, visiting tiger 'sanctuaries' and having lots of 'organised fun', I embarked on the final leg of my travels to visit my eldest sister, Tiffany, in Australia, where I was lucky enough to be present for the birth of my first niece.

Once I had completed my quest to find myself in buckets filled with unidentifiable spirits, scratchy neon 'full moon' apparel and unrequited holiday crushes, I discovered that there wasn't much to get my teeth stuck into, after all. I felt even less sure of who I was. I made so many lifelong friends on my travels, but, whilst these friendships opened my eyes to new ideas and world views, they also just underlined the fact that I, Oenone, was ill-equipped to understand myself. I didn't know what I liked, what I was good at or what my 'purpose' was.

More importantly, I was no closer to answering the question of what I wanted to study, or go on to do after higher education. Eventually, I decided based on the information that I had to hand. I picked a joint hon-ours degree in English Literature and Spanish: Spanish, because I reasoned that I was pretty much fluent any-way from my time in Ecuador; and English literature, because I had been totally in awe of, and slightly in love with, my Glaswegian English teacher. He was called Mr B, and he always wore a brown suit and tie, and I would sit right at the front of the class so as not to miss a word he said (although my school reports tended to disagree – according to them I never listened, only spoke). One time, he printed out my essay on *The Songs of Innocence and Experience* by William Blake and gave it to his classes in the year below as an exemplary piece of work. This small positive reinforcement from someone I admired formed the basis of many things for years to come, including, but not limited to, my choosing to write an essay on the same book of poems in my final year of university, professing to anyone who asked (I am sure not many did) that I was *obsessed* with William Blake and earnestly deciding to name my firstborn, whether it was a boy or a girl, Blake. That last part I am still into, sort of.

I think a lot of people pick their degrees based on metrics as extraneous as these, because what do teenagers know? What I was going to do with this degree was beyond me. Throughout school I had always naïvely assumed I would become a doctor. Coming from a medical family, I had appointed myself as a freelance medical assistant to my friends, regurgitating (probably incorrect) diagnoses for ailments and injuries, based on things my dad had said and a keen interest in *Grey's Anatomy*. My parents have photos of me flicking through copies of the *British Medical Journal* from before I could even read and I proudly asked for a nurse's watch for my sixth birthday. On underage nights out I would borrow my sister Emily's driving licence and go full method actor, assuming the role of medical student to anyone who asked me about myself in the smoking area of a nightclub. I didn't so much try to become a doctor as assume it was going to happen to me. That was until I was faced with the regrettable but undeniable truth that I had neither the natural intelligence, mental fortitude nor academic aptitude to achieve the results needed for medical school, let alone to get through a rigorous five-year medical degree. Upon this realisation I dropped my extra A level in chemistry a month before the summer exams.

So Spanish and English literature it was. With my university place secured, I could finally focus on things that really mattered, like which duvet cover set should I choose for my single bed? White sheets said grown-up, chic and classy. They are the firm choice for hotels and movies, after all, but then there was the fake tanning to consider. Then again, dark bed sheets made me feel unwell, being the territory of smelly teenage boys, so *obviously* I went with a pastel pink paisley patterned number from Primark. Cue all of my university passwords being 'paisleyduvet123' as my bed was where I spent the majority of my degree). I topped off my new foray into interior design with a big chrome Ikea lamp, which had multiple bulbs set in thick cubic glass and cast delicate shadows across the room. My flatmates and I all agreed that the lamp created great ambience and, come the evening, we often ooed and aahhed at the pure opulence of my tiny quarters.

I had animatedly pored over the freshers' essential items inventory with such delight as though it were a Hogwarts' first year supply list, rather than a catalogue of literally the most mundane objects you could ever imagine, although I did wonder whether I could forego a frying pan in favour of another stretchy mini dress for the two weeks of freshers' debauchery that I felt, very earnestly, were going to be the best of my entire life so far. I can remember with uncanny clarity all the outfits I bought in the summer sales, including an animal print body con dress from Topshop with a black mesh insert at the neckline that dipped into a deep v, creating a pleasing cleavage; a silky navy blue jumpsuit with silver buttons from Zara that was nipped in at the waist; and some black shorts made of a thick, almost curtain-like fabric from River Island.

On 17 September, my parents and I drove down to Cardiff, the car stuffed to bursting. I sat in the back, surrounded by my new world of belongings, full of excitement and nerves. My halls in Talybont North were one of the oldest. Admittedly they were a bit shabby and more run-down than the newer-built digs, but I loved them, silver fish and all. I had joined the university Facebook group and exchanged chats with others due to move into Talybont North that September. A girl from my year at school, Yas, was also arriving that day and so we decided to meet up in the afternoon. Joined at the hip after one glass of Pinot Grigio in the Student Union Bar, we were promptly – and interchangeably – christened Tweedledee and Tweedledum. Despite the fact that she was lucky enough to be in Talybont South (the posher part), she soon became a firm fixture in our dilapidated halls. Everything was broken and so old that no matter how much you scrubbed it looked scummy, which worked out in the end, because often we gave up on cleaning anyway.

We had three boys and three girls in our flat, with the same in the flat on the opposite side. We all became fast friends, leaving our front doors ajar so we could pop in and out of the flats as we pleased, not once considering that they were fire doors until we received a stern warning from a warden. We held pre-drinks almost every night with the cheapest vodka we could find, which might as well have been bleach, and two-for-a-fiver wine that burnt your throat whilst being so sickly sweet it tasted like vape liquid. Once suitably oiled, we would clatter down the staircase, warm and fuzzy, clutching cigarettes, our phones, a lip gloss and a ten-pound note, which would last us the entire evening. After popping into the Campus Social for a shot of something lurid and green, we'd teeter on into town, sometimes splashing out on a cab, splitting the five-pound fee between us.

In a more wholesome turn of events, I also took housewifery very seriously. Often, I'd attempt to host roast dinners for all twelve of us, using the ovens in the two kitchens and running between them to check on the roast potatoes, before Steph inevitably took over and saved the day. Steph and I loved each other from the moment we met. After our first night out, we shared a fag while rehashing the events of the evening before we went to bed – who had snogged who, which chip shop had been our favourite so far, what was the name of the tall guy with the nice parka? She then waited for me to go into my room so that she could vomit over the side of the balcony. This happened regularly that first week. It wasn't until day five that she informed me that she didn't smoke and that in fact it repulsed her.

It was everything I could have wished for and more. This world was miles away from the bubble that was my private school. Everybody was given a fresh start, a chance to be whoever they wanted to be, and no one judged each other for snogging, shagging, being too drunk or anything else for that matter. It was a dys-functional, messy, silly family. There were arguments and there were times when we got on each other's nerves (likely I was the most annoying), but it felt like a sort of utopia. I was so infatuated with the freedom, laughter and frivolity that I almost forgot the reason we were all there.

University is supposedly a place for education. For many, it proves to be just another extortionate hurdle towards an ever more uncertain end. For me, it was mostly about self-discovery, hedonism and experiment-ing with the liberty of adulthood. While my friends threw themselves into sporting teams, running for Athletic Union president and carving out their own corner of the library, I focussed on my favourite hobbies: buying pick 'n' mix from 'Big Tesco', getting drunk and finding a boyfriend. I perused the Harry Potter Fan Club at the Societies Fair, sauntered over to the Volleyball Soc (because the boys looked hot and the outfits cute) and I even joined the A capella Group, which, due to hangovers, I only attended twice, despite having had to audition for the spot. At one point I did consider some sort of sport, before resigning myself to the fact that it just wasn't for me. Looking back, I realise now that in my halls I was one of the few people who didn't have a definitive hobby. My romanticisation of everything had followed me into higher education, as I was waiting for the world to happen to me; for the excitement; for the drama. I thought life was one big movie and, more than anything, I wanted to fall in love; it would be good for the plot. Be careful what you wish for . . .

I started seeing someone in the spring. Let's call him X. At the end of my first year, he physically assaulted me. A group of us had gone to a club night earlier on. He didn't drink very often (I would find out later that this was why) but we were both quite tipsy and at the end of the night, when it was just us two back at his, we had a stupid, incoherent argument. I was partway through an inarticulate retort when I saw a flicker of something change in his eyes. He suddenly became enraged. Violent. I immediately sobered up. As it was happening, I remember not being able to move. I had always imagined I would be brave in this sort of situation, whatever 'brave' means, but in that moment I froze.

Afterwards I sat on the steps in the hallway of his flat, still frozen, still in shock. I called Yas and she came and drove me home. When I woke up the next morning my head was throbbing. This wasn't abnormal, I was used to hangovers, but it was a different sort of sore. It was only when the girls came in to check on me that I realised what I thought had been a nightmare was an actual memory. I rang Emily and she told me to get on the next train to London. I begged her not to tell Mum, but when I arrived at Paddington Station my mother was there, waiting for me on the platform. As soon as I saw her face I wished I had never told anyone. I didn't want it to be true; didn't want her looking at me like that. I could see the hurt, pain and anger in her eyes; knew that she thought he was a monster. I didn't see him like that at all. In fact, confusingly, I felt sorry for him; felt guilty for having made him so angry.

She took me to a hospital, told them what had happened and asked them to give me a check-up. The nurse asked me to give her his name to make a report, but I refused. Mum said the name repeatedly, pleadingly, but they said it had to come from me. I sat there tight-lipped, feeling guilty for having even let anyone know; feeling like I had already caused enough trouble. I wanted the whole thing to have never happened. I wanted everyone to forget about it. I wanted to be with him and now, by causing such a fuss, I knew I had ruined it.

That night came after the best part of a year of what one might call a 'toxic relationship', but, like so many others, after the incident I couldn't stop going back to him. I would lie to my housemates about where I was headed, making up some excuse about buying snacks or needing something from Superdrug and I'd slip away to see him. They soon caught on, but it was exhausting for them; there are only so many times you can advise someone in good faith before your patience wears thin when they don't listen. What is it they say? Doing the same thing over and over again, and expecting a different result is the first sign of madness . . . Well, I was mad with lovesickness. When we finally broke up for good, it was traumatising, messy and formative. I am sure that I listened to *Fighter* by Christina Aguilera more than anyone else in 2014. The pain from the heartbreak was physically excruciating. I had become addicted to his flawed way of loving me and couldn't figure out how to breathe without it. I would lie in bed blaring out Sam Smith to try and dampen the sound of my wails, burying my head in the pillow, my face raw from crying, nose snotty, and my hair stuck up on end like I'd just been electrocuted.

Whilst that physical altercation was certainly a punctuation mark in my early adulthood, the most significant result was not the trauma of the assault itself, but everything that it changed. When second year began, I went to so few lectures that I realised the emotional repercussions from our relationship were impacting my degree and I needed to do something about it. I visited the university counsellor who made me answer a list of questions before turning over the sheet and showing me that I had said 'yes' to all the classic signs of an abusive relationship. Not just physical, but emotional abuse, too. I was shocked. I had never loved anyone so much; never known true love like it before. How could that possibly be abuse, when it felt like I was self-harming by being away from him?

I spoke to my guidance counsellor and they decided it best I restart second year the following year, which would mean I wouldn't be back in lectures for the next ten months. I decided to change from a joint honours degree in English and Spanish to straight English literature, as I was so behind on Spanish at this point it felt too overwhelming to carry on. Now I had a long stretch to fill and this is where it all began.

I carried on living in Cardiff and decided to focus my energy on starting my heartbreak diet. It sounds so frivolous, but I was craving control after feeling so broken. I needed to regain some power, in whatever way I could, so I signed up to a six-week course with a personal trainer starting in the new year. When my alarm rang early that first week back in January, on the day of my first session, it was as though good karma herself was lodged in the bite of the cold morning air, her crisp, chilled optimism shaking me awake. The enthusiasm that propelled me to leap out of bed was foreign to every cell in my body. This new project of mine was making the previously traumatising experience of getting up in the pitch black of winter exciting and enticing. Up until now, I had been sleep's most devoted mistress, but I was leaving her at 6am, after a measly six hours together. Sometimes I would *greet* her just before sunrise, when, giggling like hyenas, myself and my friends would peel ourselves away from the dregs of a house party in the early hours. We'd slink back home stinking of booze, high on our youth and sometimes other substances, and as our mascara-encrusted eyes fought to stay open, comforted by the promise of sunrise, we'd fall hard and fast into the arms of the morning. But to get up pre-8am, like, to do stuff? Unheard of.

I was still living in the house I'd moved into at the beginning of second year. This was the first time I was awake before the others – Poppie, Steph, Yas, Kate, Katie, Issy and Becky – who lived there and who all seemed to fit seamlessly into student life. When Poppie and I first met we weren't sure about each other, both making peace with the fact that maybe we just wouldn't get along. How wrong we were. As soon as we moved in together, we fell into step with each other and have never looked back. We bonded over trashy TV, celebrity gossip, our love of clothes and our respective recent break-ups, which cemented our friendship even further. We'd lick our wounds and sanitise our broken hearts with shots of tequila and hours spent on sticky dance floors. We would flail our arms and (unrhythmically in my case) swish our hips to nineties R'n'B until we were shiny from sweat and felt exorcised of our grief.

The only problem was that Poppie was, of course, still studying, and so whilst we clung to each other in the hours outside lectures, I was listless when the girls were all at the library. Now I felt smug that I finally had something to grasp on to, given the chaos that had ensued the year before. I believed her. Kate Moss, that is. Nothing was ever going to taste as good as skinny was going to feel. It was *going* to happen and I was certain that, when it did, my whole life was going to change. No, scrap that: my whole life was just about to begin.

I pulled on my three-quarter-length, peony-pink gym leggings, a black sports bra and a black tank top, all replete with the distinctive Nike swoosh. These purchases were the result of a successful trip to Sports Direct at the beginning of my first term of uni the previous year. Never really having had a need for exercise clothing before, I had gladly signed up to the halls of residence gym along with my flatmates and used that as an excuse to go Lycra shopping – shopping being the only sport I had flirted with at this point.

I scrutinised myself in my wavy Ikea mirror, a stalwart item for my generation of students. For as long as I could remember, my reflection had been a source of contention, but that morning I scanned my shape with a fresh sensibility. Usually, all I could see was a lumpy lack of curvature, a doomed sack of potatoes, the barrier to my happy existence. Yet suddenly I felt presented with an overwhelming sense of possibility. My stomach, the part of me I despised the most, *would* flatten and harden; my thighs, sturdy but doughy and lacking in integrity, *would* become supple and sultry; and my butt *would* lift and become round like the infamous bubble butt I had heard so much about. This was science. I had seen the evidence. I had scrolled through scores of photos on Instagram of the women who had gone before me and I had witnessed them losing layers of fat, like a snake shedding its own skin. I was ready to make like a transformer and reach my final form. I had, already (miraculously, having never succeeded before) lost a little weight in anticipation of starting with my personal trainer – a bit like how my mum would make sure the apartment on holiday was spotless before the cleaner came over.

Arriving at the gym, which was a forty-minute walk from the house, I felt a mixture of excitement and trepidation. Plonked in an industrial estate on the side of a road, it wasn't an inviting edifice. The reception area was cold and stark, and through a window I could see a room filled with rusting white metal machinery. As far as I could tell, it was an old-school bodybuilding establishment, designed for tattooed, muscly men, not giggly, girly, English literature students. I was wearing a big black fur coat over my gym kit, a vintage find from a market that I'd got for Christmas a few years prior. This coat, plus my unmistakably posh English accent and embarrassing naïvety, said more than I could intuit back then. I soon realised my mistake, feeling my cheeks burning as I paid the five-pound day pass fee and asked if there was somewhere I could leave my Moira Rose-esque abomination.

Despite my self-consciousness, I didn't feel completely out of my depth amongst the machinery. Halfway through my first year, X, the ex-boyfriend who had made this course-misdirection-cum-correction happen, had introduced me to weightlifting. In fact, he was the one who introduced me to the world of bodybuilding in the first place. He would show me the basics when I swung by the hotel that he PT'd out of, usually to drop off the lunch that he had forgotten. He was the first boyfriend I'd had who seemed like a man and, as such, at the ripe old age of twenty, I was keen to impress this person who maybe one day would father my children. So, because he told me to, I started exercising. More truthfully, he told me I needed to lose weight and, instead of seeing this as a red flag, I accepted his help gladly.

He had also introduced me to the online community of bodybuilders, and I discovered the women I grew to idolise and obsess over on Instagram. White, skinny, thigh-gapped women had been the Eurocentric beauty ideal ever since I could remember. The heroin chic era of Kate Moss, Sienna Miller and their young protégées, Alexa Chung and Kaya Scodelario as Effy in *Skins*, governed my – and millions of others' – understanding of beauty. That is until female bodybuilders in the US, such as Paige Hathaway, Nikki Blackketter and Buff-Bunny (Heidi Somers), began to traverse the Atlantic Ocean via social media and beam up at me through the screen of my beloved yellow iPhone 5. Admittedly, they were also white and skinny, but in a new, muscular way. In 2023, the difference between a nineties super-model and an early fitness influencer feels like the difference between the two apparently identical belts Miranda Priestley presents to Andy in *The Devil Wears Prada*, but in 2015, when the representation of bodies on social media wasn't what it is today (and boy, do we still have a long way to go), it seemed momentously significant. Thanks to and unbeknownst to X, the tumultuous break-up that led me to seek out this six-week challenge also led to my entry into the world of influencers.

For years tabloids celebrated the way female celebrities would get smaller post break-up, glorifying how they exited a relationship and replaced their partner with a different sort of trophy: a banging body. Later, when I and a large portion of the internet were beginning to settle into a more anti-diet approach, endeavouring to educate ourselves on the body positivity and fat liberation movements, Khloé Kardashian reintroduced the phrase 'revenge body', cementing it even further into the public consciousness with her reality show, named *Revenge Body with Khloé Kardashian*. Now, talking about our bodies in a negative way is seen as sacrilegious.

It is the preserve of hushed private conversations between close friends, delivered in conscience-stricken tones and not to be repeated, especially not online. We are tying ourselves up in knots as we fight against a persistent system that demands (as close to) physical perfection as possible, whilst another force, that of rejection of the very same system, is *en vogue*.

At school my friends and I were always looking for the next fat-loss quick fix. We would devour articles in magazines exclaiming they had discovered the best 'fat-burning foods' and immediately rush to buy them. Sat on the sofa, laps laden with blueberries, goji berries and Ryvita, we would inhale these miracle snacks in quick succession whilst watching re-runs of *Friends* and wait for the fat-burning magic to happen. We were not aware of calories, nor the fact that there is no such thing as a 'fat-burning' food. We believed the more of these foods we ate, the more fat we would lose. The girls who struggled most were also the ones who weren't sporty, but for some reason we didn't equate weight loss with team sports, we equated weight loss with the gym. There was a boys' gym and a girls' gym. The boys' gym was equipped with squat racks and free weights, whilst the girls' had treadmills, Bosu balls and resistance machines. As a sport-shy girl who found group sports particularly intimidating, I often wonder whether I could have discovered the positive powers of exercise earlier had I had access to the same free weights as the boys. Our guy friends would often speak of macros, MyFitnessPal and 'gains', but we never even considered asking them what those things actually were.

Despite this, we monitored our diets and improvised our own ways to lose weight. We would starve ourselves, then inevitably binge, and then make ourselves sick or take laxatives. I once, aged seventeen, embarked on the archaic cabbage soup diet. I remember being so exhausted, grumpy and flatulent, but ecstatic that perhaps this was the answer to my prayers. A friend of mine said she had lost 'loads of weight' doing it and I thought it would be the perfect thing to try out prior to our sixth form ball. We would pass these diets around like secret family recipes, reciting instructions in earnest, with generous smiles, as though to say, 'You're welcome.' This is not to say that young children should be made hyper-aware of calories or the function of exercise in weight loss, but the problem was the lack of information back then was perhaps just as dangerous and misleading as the information teenagers can access now.

Looking back, I find all this upsetting and maddening. And worse yet, while so many of us have been through this, countless more are still going through it and will never get past it. On the podcast I later started, I spoke to the poet Charly Cox and admitted that when I was at school I used to wish that I could get into an accident that would render me virtually unharmed, but unable to eat. I'd fantasise about car crashes that resulted in a non-fatal wound to the stomach, one that wouldn't leave a terrible scar, but would mean I couldn't digest food. I would imagine myself lying in a hospital bed with nothing to do except wait for myself to literally waste away. What peace to no longer be at war with my appetite! What a relief to no longer live in fear of my body! I had never told anyone this before. I felt so ashamed and embarrassed of these dark thoughts, but as it turned out hundreds of listeners and Charly herself had had similar reveries. How utterly depressing that I had thought like this and how desperately tragic that so many others had, too.

The morning after my first gym session I woke up feeling as though I had been hit by a truck. I struggled to wash my hair due to the dull ache and heaviness of my arms, and found myself waddling around like I had just partaken in, well, let's not go there. I wasn't only exhausted from the new *physical* assault on my body, but also the calorie deficit accompanying it. The fitness programme wasn't just a training regime, but a 'full meal plan', too. This was made up of what was fundamentally one meal, divided into three tiny meals and a snack. Dismally, my favourite part was the post-workout protein shake, which, after dry chicken wrapped in lettuce with a zero-calorie dressing, *almost* resembled something tasty. It was one scoop of chocolate protein powder with a handful of frozen berries and water, blended. I'd wash it down with a Marlboro Gold.

Every Sunday morning, after nipping to the bathroom – but careful not to eat or even let a drop of water pass my lips – I would stand in my underwear and employ one of my housemates to take my progress photos. Front, side and back. I would try to stand as straight as possible, my posture immaculate and my face deathly serious, like I was shooting lingerie mug shots. My 'progress' was visible from the very first week and this marker of success gave me the ambition I needed. It was going to work this time. After nearly a decade of trying, I was going to get there.

Running had never interested me, not least because of the cigarettes and all-nighters, but also because it required a mental robustness that I didn't seem to possess. I had never had much resilience when it came to extra-curricular activities and I would often quit things at the slightest hurdle. My therapist would later tell me that my core belief about myself is that there is something wrong with me. So, for much of my life, whenever that was confirmed, I never challenged it. I believed that I was bad at everything that I wasn't immediately talented at. And on that front, the only things I seemed to have a natural flair for were being told off, failed relationships and repeatedly going over my overdraft limit. Oddly, this gave me a serene lack of fear when it came to failure, because I expected it anyway, but it also meant I was never good at trying when the going got tough.

My insecurities around exercise were largely due to the culture of body shaming and policing that I grew up in, plus the fact that I went to a ridiculously sporty private school. Renowned for its sporting alumni, including a number of today's Premiership rugby players and a not insignificant number of Olympians, if you weren't confident in the exercise department, then it wasn't the best place to foster a sense of security. With gazelle-like hurdlers, county champion runners and burgeoning gold medallists, it was an intimidating environment for someone whose natural lack of spatial awareness meant they were eternally covered in bruises from walking into their bed frame at least once a day.

When I was at school, diet culture was a way of life. Even then, when I had barely started to develop, I wanted to be physically smaller, but, ironically, my internalised fatphobia also acted as a barrier to taking on most forms of exercise. I found the idea of people seeing me huffing and puffing absolutely mortifying. I could imagine the flesh of my legs curdling as my feet struck the floor, like mismeasured cake batter, sending a ricochet of cellulite up my thighs. The bodybuilding gym was undoubtedly intimidating, but felt safer, less exposing and more nurturing than my previous forays into movement, but, rather than the most well-equipped sporting school in the country, I have Instagram to thank for my eventual athletic confidence, because, even though in hindsight my weight loss was unhealthy, through social media I was becoming empowered by the knowledge I was gaining from bodybuilders and fitness Instagrammers. Whilst the onus was still on weight loss, fat loss and ultimately becoming as lean as possible, at least the science was, for the most part, correct.

As I delved deeper into the world of female body-builders, I started to feel slightly more at peace with my own shape. Their legs were lean but meaty, their stomachs flat but without hip bones that jutted out, and, overall, their bodies somewhat looked like mine. I realised I'd never related to Effy, Kate Moss or the supermodels that graced the catwalks, but I saw something of myself in these new aspirational figures. Even though these women were still 'thin', it felt like a huge leap in terms of which bodies were acceptable and which weren't.

Paying a personal trainer added another important component to my lifelong quest for thinness: accountability. Having never truly 'invested' in anything before, I took the whole process very seriously. To my surprise, I seemed to have a knack for it and, even more shockingly to me, within a couple of weeks of starting the six-week challenge, I got the bug for exercise. Whilst weight training is intense and difficult, it is broken up into chunks, with the actual exertion lasting only minutes if not seconds. Compared to the cardio I had tried, tested and detested, it was not only manageable, but enjoyable. The humiliation I usually felt being triggered by any sort of physical exercise didn't seem to penetrate through the stern purposeful building. A space designed for raw power, sweat and probably quite a lot of steroid use was to become somewhere to incubate my self-confidence, if not entirely, then at least when it came to my ability to take on physically challenging tasks.

My parents, unsure of what to make of their youngest daughter living away from home but no longer studying, were on the phone almost every day, asking where I would be working and how I would be filling my time. By this point I was working at a restaurant in town most days (having been fired from the nightclub where Yas and I had worked for the past two years – I can't remember why, but I respect their decision), but, understandably, my parents wanted me to have something to show for the time that I was, in their eyes, whiling away. None of us could have predicted, least of all them, what was to come. Seeing results week after week was addictive, rewarding and to me felt almost biblical. I was reaching highs, or rather lows (of body fat), I could never have imagined. And in those days, to me and much of the world, that equated to hotness. I was the hottest I had ever been and unless you've been living a very blissfully ignorant life under a rock, I am sure you will be aware that hotness is a very potent thing to possess in our society: it changes everything.

When I first moved from the bodybuilding gym to the local easyGym, I felt intimidated by all the people in the weights section, a phenomenon so common it has its own term: gymtimidation. I had only ever trained in the quiet hotel gym with X or in the secluded bodybuilding gym accompanied by my PT, whereas the local gym was full of students and Cardiff locals. The weights section was populated by burly, grunting men, who'd sooner eat their own arm than give up the ever-coveted squat rack. Not confident enough to take up space without a male companion in tow, I would drag all seven of my housemates along with me, getting them to create a human shield around the apparatus. At the end of my session, as payment, I would take us to the mats and lead a rudimentary legs, bums and tums circuit.

Alongside the habit of regular exercise, I had tangentially formed another habit. I had begun to post on Instagram. And I posted a lot. Initially, I made separate private accounts in the hope that no one who knew me IRL would find me and think I was 'up myself'. To begin with, I only told my housemates about these accounts, mortified at the thought of my school friends finding them and taking the piss out of me. Which, *obviously*, they eventually did. Very unsubtly, might I add. (It's ok, everyone is an egomaniac online nowadays, so, again, I was just accidentally ahead of the curve!)

I can't remember exactly when I got the guts to go public with my account, but it was certainly a deviation from the smoking, singing, PE-skipping class clown that many would have recognised me as. The new me was disciplined, seemingly knowledgeable and manically smiley. Fitness people are always smiley. It could be the happy lifestyle, the lack of hedonism or simply the constipation-induced trapped wind. I was constipated a lot back then. It was also the face of the moment, before next-gen cool girls swapped smiles for 'lobotomy-chic': 'the performance of detachment – to look as though you just happened to be photographed whilst contemplating your abject disaffection with the world around you'.[1] When I was starting out, if my head was in the picture, so was every single one of my teeth, but never mind lobotomy chic, most fitness pages back then preferred full decapitation, with seas of torso-filled images flooding the explore pages, so we will never know who was smiling and who was pouting.

My page was about health, happiness and how to soft-boil an egg. I was earnestly trying to become the sort of woman that drank green smoothies at 6am, always had a glowing tan and worked out twice a day. I was posting quotes that read, 'Abs are made in the kitchen', 'The best time to start is now' and 'You can't out-train a bad diet'. Heroin chic was out, clean living was in. It looked like the world of beauty was making a change for the better and I wanted to be a part of it. It is plain as day now that both camps were pumping themselves full of non-essential products, eating not nearly enough and focussing entirely too much on women's bodies and very little else, but on the outside, and to me, it felt like a revolution.

This passion project was oddly grounding. I was twenty-one, at a point where everything felt like it was balanced on a tightrope, and I still had absolutely no idea what I wanted to do with my life. Like an ant

---

[1] 'The cult of the dissociative pout', Rayne Fisher-Quann, *i-D*, May 2022.

scuttling around at random to find the shade, I had thrown my efforts into so many different avenues over the years, not once landing in a spot that offered me sufficient shelter, until my little page started to grow and provided a nourishing habitat in which I felt I could flourish. It seemed that I was good at it, even if I wasn't entirely sure what 'it' was.

Although I didn't realise it at the time, the reward was the obvious – it was dopamine from the likes, follows and comments. I, less cynically, had the sweet and somewhat guileless belief that I was helping people. The idea that my minuscule twenty-one-year-old body was somehow changing the world, one striation at a time, buoyed me to keep going, to share online in spite of my fears and insecurities. I could overcome my ego if it meant I was somehow useful to other people, I thought, not appreciating that what I was doing was feeding my ego. To give myself a smidge of credit, I do think I shared interesting and useful information, it's just outdated now and slightly cringe. In the nostalgic age of the – devastatingly departed – chronological Instagram feed (RIP), it was socially acceptable, encouraged even, to upload a play by play of your day. My feed consisted of – mostly headless – selfies. I would love to call these 'belfies' like a 'belly selfie', but a 'belfie' is actually a bum selfie and, unfortunately, I posted a lot of those as well, alongside motivational quotes and photos and videos of my soft-boiled eggs #yolkporn.

This was the era of CleanEatingAlice, GraceFitUK, Deliciously Ella et al., when a moniker was way more in fashion than your actual name. I tried on a few for size. Sat on the loo in our third-year uni house, with the door open to our galley kitchen where my housemates were cooking and babbling away to each other, I announced I was 'rebranding' to @thetinytank. Clearly, somewhere in my subconscious, I was aware that I was about to build a brand and that the name was important. First was @fitnessforbat, then @healthyhappynoni, then @thetinytank, then post-fitness influencing years @uhnonee and finally just @oenone . . . not much unlike @beyoncé, ahem. A year before landing on @thetinytank, I had been in the kitchen of my previous student house and exclaimed, in what many may now call #manifesting, that 'One day I am going to be one of those girls that gets sponsored by Nike and paid to work out.'

By 2016, even though I was back to studying again, I had become a regular easyGym goer, often going twice a day. Whilst I had stopped snoozing my alarm, some old habits die hard. I would have a cigarette pre- and post-workout, puffing away outside the gym at 6am before doing Tabata sprints on the treadmill. This is an intense sort of interval training consisting of twenty seconds of activity and then ten seconds off for eight rounds, which I would do for twenty minutes. I couldn't do that now even if you paid me, let alone after a Marlboro Gold. Despite this filthy habit, or perhaps in part thanks to it (cigarettes being a well-known appetite suppressant), I had sustained a level of leanness for some time. After a while, I started to get men approaching me in the gym to ask me if I was going to do a competition. What competition you ask? Bikini, of course. I knew exactly what they meant, as lots of my idols were professional competitors, so rather than lament the audaciousness of men, I was flattered. For the uninitiated, it follows this format: you stand on stage wearing only an extortionately glittery bikini, see-through stripper heels that cut your toes to pieces and a spray-tan that quite frankly qualifies as blackfishing. To showcase your physique, you contort yourself into such exaggerated poses that you feel like your external organs are going to escape through your mouth. I decided to sign up.

Like every other challenge I took on, I left everything to the last minute. In fact, I took just six weeks to get stage lean. It was the amount of time it had taken me to get ludicrously lean with my PT and with that being all I had to go off, that was the timeframe I gave myself. This is not par for the course. For the competition, however, I managed to get even more miniscule. I looked gaunt. My clothes hung off my hips, my shoulders jutted out as well as being oddly globular and all my facial features looked cartoonish. I remember thinking I looked fantastic. I completely lost my libido, was so exhausted that I had to nap every day and, of course, I was starving. So starving, that in order to try and stop myself eating straight from the 5kg tub of Myprotein unsalted (vom) peanut butter (the only thing left in my cupboards approximating a snack), I decided to put it in the freezer. Cut to me stood in my pyjamas at 2am, huge knife in hand, hacking away at the icy brown lump. I would not recommend a bikini competition, but frozen peanut butter is actually delicious. You should try it.

In the run-up to the competition I met Abby, one half of the duo @gains4girls with her (now our) friend Lucy, who at this point were much 'bigger' on Instagram than I was. We started following each other, spoke on Instagram DMs and realised we were taking part in the same competition that coming April. We discussed bikini colour, type of shoe, what jewellery we were going to wear, how we were going to do our makeup and style our hair, but mostly we spoke elaborately, almost pornographically, about all the food we would eat afterwards. Abby is a fantastic baker to this day, and I can vividly remember her telling me about the Biscoff-laden cookies and Nutella-packed treats she would be bringing along with her, and salivating at the thought.

My best friends, my mum and Yas's mum all came to my competition. Abby brought her friends along who all had accounts with varying numbers of followers: @gains4girls, @gracefituk, @emlouisefit, @annafituk and I, @thetinytank, would soon become close pals, and negotiate the uncertain terrain of influencing together. Anxious and antsy, I smoked ferociously beforehand, sweating my fake tan off on the unseasonably hot April morning, so much so that the inside of my arms were completely white, I resembled a baby deer and I had to be re-sprayed. After the competition, we all went back to Yas's parents' house in Portsmouth, not far from where the event was held. Her mum, Maria, had put on the most incredible spread you could possibly imagine: think feast at Hogwarts. I ate so much my stomach ballooned into a basketball and I had to lie prone on the sofa for fear of vomiting if I stood up. My belly ached and strained and protested as it tried to take on the gargantuan meal thrust upon it after such prolonged starvation. I, too, felt like shit. My gut and I were having a strop in unison.

Miraculously I had placed fifth. However, due to not understanding how sport works, I hung up my bikini and retired from competing the minute I got off stage. I hadn't realised my placement meant I was supposed to go on to further rounds of the competition. Back in Cardiff, I struggled, like every other participator in such competitions, with the inevitable weight gain. Watching myself grow back to a healthy weight was harder than getting into that shape in the first place. I constantly posted throwbacks on my Instagram, with promises that I would start to 'cut' (gym speak for diet) soon. I would often post the same pre-comp photo over and over again, and each time it gained tens of thousands of likes, whilst I had fewer than ten thousand followers (a feat almost impossible now). I was sure that I would get back to bikini weight and stay there forever, and this narrative fed my Instagram as I diarised how I would get there, how anyone could get there. I had the golden ticket.

At this point in time there was no such thing as an influencer as we understand the term today. Some people may have had tens of thousands of followers and be making money from adverts, but no one had millions and there was no regulation. People would engage in real time, under each other's posts, and friendships were formed with people both near and far. At each successive stage of life it gets more and more difficult to make friends, so this was exciting. You could purposefully find like-minded people and reach out to them. Instagram felt like an online journal for the world to read. Of course, there had been Myspace, then Bebo, then Facebook, the difference being that those online places were designed for people who were already friends or groups of people you had met in real life. On Instagram it wasn't too awkward to follow along with a stranger's life, whereas it would have felt slightly alien on other sites, except for maybe Tumblr, but Tumblr was mostly anonymous. I had used Tumblr and Reddit a bit when I was at school, always in secret. I would go on to pro-ana (pro-anorexia) websites and bookmark black and white images of girls with thigh gaps adorned with quotes fetishising starvation, but this was never a hobby to be shared.

Instagram felt less dark and peripheral than these sites. It was more optimistic, especially in the fitness space.

These women and men looked gorgeous and achieved it through life-enhancing techniques: gymming, running and yoga, paired with tanned skin, green smoothies and perfect eggs. Filters didn't exist in the way that they do now and unless they were adept at Adobe Photoshop it was unlikely that your lay person was editing their bodies or faces in the way that we see now. Even then, though, I would agonise for hours about the appearance of my body in photos. The goal would be to eradicate every wrinkle, dimple and roll, which I would do painstakingly through contorting myself, stretching and shrinking along planes of motion to smooth my stomach, elongate my legs and round my bum. I would try on all of my friends' underwear, searching for the perfect combination of sexy but not lewd. A pair of Yas's Jack Wills full briefs became my pant of choice; they weren't lingerie, they had a girl-next-door feel and they didn't seem to try too hard. In fact, poor Yas's wardrobe featured on my Instagram feed more than it did on her body during this era. I would diligently tap away on my iPhone 5 evening after evening, my tongue escaping the corner of my mouth in concentration as I agonised over fitting my point into the limited caption box, often eagerly spilling over into the comments section. I remember the adrenaline rush as I hit post and immediately saw the likes and comments rolling in. That was when I had fewer than ten thousand followers and the proverbial pond of the platform was small enough for there to be a real sense of community. It was truly the golden age of Instagram for content creators: we were raw, reactive and first generation. I remember going to sleep with my stomach flipping as I watched my posts get thousands of likes in real time. And then I would wake up to a home screen that looked like it had just popped a pinger at Reading Festival. Notification after notification after notification after notification after notification after notification after notification. Yes, it was exhausting. And exhilarating. And addictive.

Whether you are beautiful, your home is beautiful or your clothes are beautiful, beauty is integral to creating, curating and sustaining a social media presence on photo- or video-based platforms. If I am honest with myself – and you – then almost everything I ever did up until my early twenties was overshadowed by my unwavering pursuit of beauty. From as young as eleven, I had absorbed an understanding of the power of beauty. I viewed it as a prerequisite for being valued and I had resolved to make sure I had some, not necessarily with the end goal of being supremely beautiful, but more in terms of living up to expectations. Most of the time I don't think I'm pretty and, much like everyone else, I find it hard to be sure how everyone else sees me, but at the same time I *know* that my 'prettiness' *is* a part of how people see me, even though I can't always see it myself. And even if you don't think I'm pretty, my whiteness, blue eyes and blonde hair, along with my accent, mean that society is mostly kind to me when it sees and hears me. But when I was younger, I equated beauty almost entirely with thinness. This meant that above all else, my biggest desire, day in day out, was to somehow become 'skinny'.

So it was social media that ironically gave me the tools to eventually overcome my disordered eating and body image issues. Through meeting and engaging with like-minded women and men, all embarking on a pilgrimage to organised and approved starvation, I managed to climb out the other side, unscathed and more healed than I was when I went in. I had to go through the period of Tupperware boxes lined up in the fridge, like soldiers, ready to be called forward for the day's battle against hunger; alarms set to ever earlier to forge extra time for sweating; paraphernalia and apparatus to weigh both what was to be consumed and the consumer – little scoops for protein and other superfluous powders, gigantic water bottles, the size of a very large baby and shaped a bit like a dumbbell. I had to go through all that to get to where I am now, which is, more or less apathetic towards my diet. I think about food when I am eating or when I am hungry, but I never ruminate on meals past or fret about meals to come. It is, when I write it down like that, quite extraordinary.

This journey to recovery began because, despite everything I was posting on my page, after my competition normal life had to resume and normal life, it turned out, was much more enjoyable. I wouldn't be truly 'healed' until a few years later, but I was through the worst of it. I had reached the apex of what my physique could do and when I reached the summit, do you know what was at the top? When I was the leanest I could physically be, at one point aided by eating an inordinate amount of asparagus in order to harness the vegetable's diuretic power and completely dehydrate me for my competition? Absolutely nothing. Worse than nothing. You may look like an 'athlete', but unless all you want is to be a mannequin, it is no way to live. I started to drink again and go on nights out with my friends, something I hadn't done for a while. I went out for meals and took rest days. My clothes fit me properly. I had energy and a social life. I felt happier and healthier. I had all the things I thought I had been seeking before, when actually I had just been seeking thinness. (I couldn't eat asparagus for months after that, even though it's one of my top three favourite vegetables.)

Unfortunately, for the most part the paradigms of beauty championed on social media mirror our structurally racist, ableist, fatphobic society. So, it's no wonder that there was a time when Instagram was almost synonymous with fitness content. Skinny, 'toned', blonde women like me were ten a penny, but valued as much more by the algorithm. I had accidentally tapped into the goldmine. Even if I wasn't sustaining an abnormally low body fat, I still had abs and quads and that 'gym look'. More importantly, I had had a weight loss transformation, and those before and after pictures, the ones that brought new followers every time I shared them, were my meal ticket. I just didn't know it yet.

Chapter 2

I STARTED 2017 with another break-up. I had met Y in the spring of 2015 and by the autumn we were 'Facebook official'. Once again, my taste in men proved itself to be less than satisfactory. This time, the relationship imploded when I found Instagram DMs from Y to another girl, whom he had dated a bit before me. On Valentine's Day, no less. I had been uploading a picture of us to his Instagram story on his phone and, as I was doing so, a message from her popped up on the screen. I clicked on it absentmindedly and as my eyes scanned its contents, my heart began to thump with anxiety, and my chest and cheeks became very hot.

I immediately locked myself in my bedroom with the jeroboam of prosecco from Aldi that we were supposed to be enjoying together that evening. I ignored Y as he banged on the door, pleading for an opportunity to explain himself. With one shaking hand I messaged the girl and with the other swigged straight from the bottle. She apologised, saying she hadn't realised we were still together, offering her sympathy and promising that nothing had happened beyond what I had seen. She was a girl's girl, I thought; a small consolation for the absolute betrayal I felt coursing through my body.

Eventually, after some time – it could've been minutes, but it felt like hours – Y stopped begging. I heard the front door to the flat slam shut. I rang Poppie. 'We need to go out!' I garbled down the phone. I tried to explain the situation, but my words were jumbled and my mind racing. Luckily, although it was a Tuesday, Poppie, like me, will never let you down if you need to dance. By the time she arrived, my reserves of tears were depleted, but I had replaced all the liquid in my body with cheap bubbly. We planned to go to my favourite night – Revs – my favourite because it was the dressiest of all the student nights, meaning you could wear high heels instead of trainers. I peeled off the red three-piece lingerie set I had been wearing underneath my long black dress. It was the first time I had worn underwear like that. 'He didn't even get to see it,' I thought to myself as I shoved my bra and knickers back in my drawer. I reapplied my make-up, careful to conceal the red blotches scattered across my face and chest from the heat rash that had accompanied my laboured sobs. I selected a stretchy navy body suit, tight black trousers and a trusty pair of nude Primark heels. I slicked my hair back into a ponytail and finished the look with a pair of big, sparkling, dangly earrings.

The night was a blur. I woke up early the next day and had a moment of serene bliss before the memory of the night before slammed into my consciousness. Anger flared up inside me once more. I talked to my sister, Emily, who declared that the best thing to do would be to shame him. Men get away with this behaviour all too often, she said, and I should use the power and tools at my disposal to expose him. I considered this and, after some deliberation and a desire for vengeance, I posted a meme to my Instagram, which read, 'It's better to have a friend with 2 chins, than a friend with 2 faces.' It was black text on a plain white background and in the caption I explained, in a vague sort of way, what had happened and that I stood with any other woman who had been through or was going through this.

Under my post, scores of comments rolled in. Initially, I replied to each one with gusto, allowing myself to get into long protracted conversations about how all men are trash and offering my sympathy to the women who had also been betrayed or cheated on, often in more extreme ways than I myself had been. There were mothers sharing tales of their husbands leaving them in the dead of night for another woman, never to be seen again; women my age who'd caught their boyfriend by snooping through their phones; and girls going through their first double betrayal after finding out their boyfriend had kissed their friend in a club.

My student bedroom became stuffy as I festered in my pyjamas, unwashed, hungover and emotionally drained, but spurred on by the support from these online strangers. The post amassed over three hundred comments, something that I would consider quite an extraordinary number today. It garnered so much momentum, in fact, that it lifted me out of my devastation for a little bit.

The following morning I deleted the caption, saying I never wanted to leave it there permanently. I think I felt a bit guilty about it, but the community support that had been readily available when I needed it was truly remarkable. I felt like all these (mostly) women who followed me really had my back. This was a two-way relationship: I was engaging with them every waking hour, sharing as much knowledge as I could on health and exercise, and in return they were there when I needed them, too. Nothing ignites a community like drama. If you really want to build a following, an easier (although never guaranteed) route to rapid numbers is to fuel controversy, or to always have a hot take, or to let your life play out in real time, warts and all. It was like I was running my own reality show, playing the part of protagonist, editor and director. The setting was Cardiff University. The plot? A student figuring out her life. The storyline? Raw, undulating and fundamentally entertaining relationship woes meets student life meets weight loss journey.

I had shared Y on social media a lot. He had liked doing cute little stories with me and being a part of my profile. He was tall, handsome and made me laugh, and I had been proud of how funny he was. I had wanted to show him off and enjoyed sharing our relationship. I had adored his willingness to join me in an online space that had for so long been somewhere only I inhabited; a place where fierce self-belief was in constant battle with even more ferocious self-doubt, in a world where I felt I needed boyfriends to cosign not only my reality, but now my digital persona, too.

Perhaps a more secure person would never have found themselves so invested in providing for strangers on the internet, dedicating hours of their time to cultivating an audience. Nowadays, when the potential payoffs are so clear and the concept so routine it wouldn't be odd for any type of person to strive to grow a following, but back then it wasn't your everyday. There was no real point to any of it. I have always been outgoing, seemingly confident and never a wallflower, but I also could be sullen, insecure and struggle in social situations. I found that lots of the girls (and we were, for all intents and purposes, girls back then) I met doing the same as me were much shyer in reality than their happy-go-lucky YouTube and Instagram alter egos. These were people more comfortable making content at home for thousands to view online than heading out to parties. I used to find it slightly paradoxical, but it makes total sense to me now.

That break-up, then, was messy. I had blocked him on everything, but it still dragged on for months, each time with him only reconfirming, on multiple occasions, what I already knew to be true. I went back again and again until we well and truly ran the relationship into the ground. After that experience, I promised myself that, from now on, once a relationship was over, I would walk away before it burned into something unrecognisable from the love on which it was once built. I am notoriously bad at learning my lessons, but this one I have managed to take in.

This also changed the landscape of my online world. I didn't realise it at the time, but quite apart from the information I shared in my captions – information that I agonised over and spent ages researching – covering subjects from muscle gain to healing your relationship with food, my following was growing because I was an open book, a chronic over-sharer, naïve to the permanence of the internet. My honesty was rewarded by likes, follows and loyalty, from scores of women who saw something in my vulnerability that they could relate to alongside my aspirational fitness content.

Did I just say I am bad at learning lessons? Sure enough, I had another very public online break-up with Z at the start of 2022. Z was my first truly serious boyfriend. We were together for four years and lived together for almost two. Our break-up was amicable, but inevitable. Nothing went wrong, we were in many ways 'the perfect couple', but it just wasn't working.

One Sunday, after cooking a roast dinner, we sat down to eat and I looked up at him and said, 'I'm not happy.' 'I know,' he replied. We had come to this road bump before, never quite daring to cross it, but I knew that this time, if we were going to break up, it had to be for real. Instead of immediately crumbling, we ate, chatted, and allowed our words to dance around the cloud from the nuclear bomb I had just detonated in both our lives. I always think one of the hardest parts of leaving a relationship is severing yourself from your shared possible future. You aren't just leaving the person you've been with for four years, but the forty years ahead you've subconsciously constructed in your mind. I remember I'd read an article that said the longer an unhappy relationship is, the more you struggle to leave it, because you've invested so much time you want to see a return on that investment, usually marriage or a family, even though in the present moment you know that it isn't working and you'd probably be better off apart. It had been so hard to peel ourselves away from each other, because everything looked and seemed right.

I moved on to the sofa. I messaged my mum, sisters and five of my closest friends, knowing that telling people outside us would set things into motion and cement the truth of the decision. Distributing the weight of this failure felt relieving and oddly numbing. Our friends and families were shocked when we told them we were breaking up. To everyone else, our 'us' made sense. Except, it didn't. Not really. Not at all. Not anymore. Not for a while.

Unsettlingly, my mind then began to wonder, anxiously, whether to share this on my social media platform. After all, that 'everyone else' also included my Instagram following. Did I even need to announce it? My following wasn't *that* big, but then I did share Z on my page and I personally would have found it weird if I didn't say anything. I pushed this dilemma to the back of my mind until the following day, when I found the flat that I would eventually move into two months later. I was tearing through this break-up process at break-neck speed with the knowledge that if I let myself stop, even for just a second, I might just retreat back into the comfort of our ill-fitting safety blanket relationship. I didn't want that. I wanted it to be clean, neat and as painless as possible. I wanted us to cut ourselves equally down the middle, so we would both be left whole when we ultimately walked away, rather than having to untangle months of 'will we, won't we' and everything that I knew came with protracted break-ups.

I decided I would do it, the announcement, when I moved out of our shared flat. I would post a story about my new place saying, 'New year, new home'. Then I would do some talking-to-camera stories about our break-up. I imagined all of this in granular detail; how I would deliver the information, whilst making sure I phrased things with grace, careful to be generous and kind to Z, as he had been throughout our relationship.

As it transpired, no amount of mental gymnastics, boundaries or offline processing would shield me from other people's opinions. I would learn that no matter what I did, I wouldn't be allowed to control the narrative. Somewhat dishearteningly, although perhaps obviously, I do not have the power to influence every single person who follows me to be supportive. Or even to be kind.

When the time came to do 'the announcement', as I was referring to it in my head (like I was a politician about to make a public formal statement about education reform, rather than the very routine phenomenon of a twenty-something choosing to no longer be with another twenty-something), I felt so anxious I couldn't actually speak. I felt wobbly and flushed and totally out of sorts. I was nervous to admit that we hadn't been able to make it work. I felt a sort of shame at this perceived failure. I had waited for two months, specifically so that I *would* be ready. In the end I decided to write it down instead. I penned a brief couple of paragraphs on my stories, detailing the fact that we had split, that it was amicable and that, although it was difficult, I was ok.

Again, the overwhelming outpouring of love I received from my followers was, well, overwhelming. The kindness, vulnerability and generosity of their words, sharing with me their own break-up stories or reassuring me that I would be ok came as a total relief. There were thousands of them. I had forgotten that social media could be like this; that I wasn't just speaking into the ether. I had let it lose its sparkle in my mind, but what I thought would be the final punctuation mark in what I was viewing as our 'conscious uncoupling' was done. My audience were the last thing carrying the ghost of our relationship and now I was unburdened of that, too. I know this sounds super-melodramatic, but that is how it felt at the time.

I had done the right thing, though, both in my private and online lives. For the first time, the break-up process was clean. Z and I even stayed friends: he sent me a Gorillas order when I said I hadn't eaten as I had been trying to do DIY all day and asked me for my advice on where to get second-hand furniture. I felt like not only had I mastered break-ups, but I had also finally learnt how to balance what to share, what not to share and when to do it. Social media is, like most things, a waltz. It looks like some simple steps to learn, but the better you get at it, the more you learn the rhythms and become adept at not stepping on anyone's toes.

Oddly, during that period between splitting up and me posting online about it, I felt like I was leading a double life. I was almost willing my audience to ask me where he was or if we were still together, but nobody seemed to notice that he didn't feature on my feed anymore. Waiting for my self-imposed deadline to creep up on me, so I could get on with things without feeling as though I was lying by omission, I wondered whether I was irrelevant now, but this was what I had wanted. I had made a vow to keep this relationship relatively private, precisely so that should the time ever come when we were no longer together I would have the space to heal in private. I recently read an article in the *New York Times* about content creators suffering from burnout after years of sharing their lives online.[2] One creator said his therapist had taught him to, 'Share from the scar, not the wound.' Giving myself those eight weeks to grieve and process my relationship offline and out of sight was exactly that. I was strong enough to share it with my audience without finding questions or comments about it invasive or upsetting.

Or so I thought. A couple of weeks after I moved out, he started seeing someone else. I found out straight away. Days after this we were due to celebrate my book deal and he had booked my favourite restaurant for the occasion. Even though we weren't together anymore, it still felt right that we commemorate my biggest career achievement to date. We had had it in the diary for months, but with this new information I didn't know if I felt ready to see him. I needed a bit of time to adjust. I suggested we cancel the reservation, go another time perhaps. 'I think I'll still go,' he responded. That night, he took her instead. This felt like a punch to the gut;

---

[2] 'Young Creators are Burning Out and Breaking Down', Taylor Lorenz, *New York Times*, June 2021.

disrespectful even. He fervently disagreed. And so, it all changed. I'd naïvely thought we'd be best friends after the break-up, as we had been friends before we were ever together, but that became impossible when he started sharing their relationship. He had been with me through so much of my career that I thought he really understood the way social media worked, and how important it was to be cautious and careful when it came to what to share and when. Far be it for me to dictate what he posted. After all, more people have seen me in my underwear than the capacity of the O2 Arena, but I thought out of respect he would have given the break-up more room to breathe. Instead, he posted more frequently than he ever had before. People started to tag me in his new girlfriend's posts, DM me her account or otherwise speculate about our break-up on gossip websites. I was not only humiliated for myself, but also for her. What did she think of this?

I also found it frustrating. I thought I had done all the right things in order to handle the whole thing privately and respectfully. I cared that he was – intentionally or not – feeding the trolls and some of the crueller comments were starting to get to me. They were starting to make me feel paranoid. 'That's not my problem,' was his reply when I asked him if he could, as a friend, refrain a little. This also came as a shock.

I had been the happiest I'd been in ages. I loved my new flat and I was spending more time with my friends than ever, free from the constraints of a relationship I had outgrown and organising my life on my own terms. I felt like I was really becoming a woman, finding my place in the world and about to embark on a new chapter of self-discovery. And yet some faceless strangers on the internet wanted me to be hurting, not happily enjoying my new freedom, and Z had gone from being my closest confidante and support to someone who was fuelling the fire – or so it felt.

It shouldn't have affected me so much, but it really did. I became overcome with fear, more insular and more private online than I had ever been. I started sharing photos of nights out only, never anything vulnerable or too personal. I suddenly felt like I was under surveillance and that if I showed any sign of weakness it would be used against me. Of course, you might be thinking that I was indeed under surveillance. I had over one-hundred thousand people following me at that point. The truth is, it had felt like a community and a safe space, like we were in it together. Not anymore. Even a full six months after we had called it quits, when I had well and truly moved on, I was still getting comments like, 'So cringe how desperate you are to show Z that you're living your "best life" *laughing crying face emoji*'

After a pretty straightforward and painless break-up, I found myself dealing with a different sort of heartbreak. It was a huge turning point in my relationship with social media. I began to question everything. Did I deserve this? Why did these people want to hurt me?

Why did they care this much? I realised that, in a way, I was being punished for my lack of vulnerability, for dealing with my personal life in private. For not hurting publicly. When you have been online for as long as I have, some people – admittedly, in my case, a small minority – can feel entitled to more of you than you're willing to give. It can feel like a betrayal when context or insight isn't provided, and so they will construct their own with whatever information they can find. And because I only existed on their phone, it was very easy to channel anger and frustration, and project them on to me. As much as they felt like they knew me, I was not really *real* in their mind. They might have had access to me, formed a relationship with me and felt connected to me in some way, which I did, too, to a lot of my followers, but over time I have created boundaries around that access, which, whilst undeniably healthy for me as an individual, can be damaging for Oenone *the brand*. There isn't really a right to reply when it comes to online trolling. Not literally, of course. I could defend myself to the hilt if I so wished, but as Oscar Wilde said, 'Don't feed the trolls; nothing fuels them so much.' When I see completely made-up remarks about myself or my friends online, I have to keep schtum. If I react or try to set the record straight, they only double down gleefully. Their anonymity grants them the freedom to say whatever they want, no matter how hurtful, vindictive or untrue.

This is a really tough pill to swallow. It is only a very

small portion of people who create fake accounts without profile pictures or comment on anonymous websites and rationally I should be able to accept this, but when your livelihood is dependent on people liking and supporting you, it's hard not to view it as a much greater threat than it really is. I have been subject to sporadic trolling throughout my career, sometimes much crueller than it was in this instance, but it never cut as deep as it did when I realised that I might be craving a life incompatible with what it takes to be a successful influencer, the only consistent career I had had thus far and one that I felt I was pretty good at. When I started out, I willingly shared every aspect of my life. I hadn't acknowledged that in doing so I was making a deal with the devil. Should I later want to keep some things to myself, that would come with a price.

Now I understand that this merging of the self into a 'brand' means we enter into a strange symbiotic relationship with our work. And this is why it hurts. It becomes almost impossible not to take things personally. Jia Tolentino wrote in her collection of essays, *Trick Mirror*, that social media has blurred the boundaries between private and public, personal and professional. For influencers, everything we do becomes work. You could say that every time we try, consume, talk about or otherwise interact with anything that is purchasable, we are working. After all, isn't that market research, with the chance to post about it online? Then again, maybe we can all say that now? The way late-stage capitalism operates on us, we constantly consume, share and seek out our next product – from food to clothes to experiences – which means we are almost always on and in some way contributing to the economy, even if we aren't being paid to do so. Tolentino writes, 'Capitalism has no land left to cultivate but the self. Everything is being cannibalized – not just goods and labor, but personality and relationships and attention. The next step is complete identification with the online marketplace, physical and spiritual inseparability from the internet,' and, she says, it's 'a nightmare that is already banging down the door.'

It's possible she's right. In fact, of course she is, but as I am so inside the beast, so of the beast, I don't know if I find it as terrifying as she makes it feel. It just feels . . . normal. Often, it's subconscious, we (influencers) may take an action for ourselves and, because it is second nature for us to do so, we post about it. Every now and then, something seemingly innocuous will see a spike in audience interaction or a bump in followers and, whether it's chemical or calculated, that thing may soon then metamorphose from something for us to something for you. We accrue more skills in that area, learn how to utilise it to our advantage and occasionally lose the joy that made us want to do it in the first place. This sounds much more deliberate than it usually is, but the outcome is the same, irrespective of intention.

Sometimes the merging can be really rewarding. During the pandemic I took up painting as something to do, posting my multi-coloured acrylic flowers with words sprawled over the top on my stories. I lamented the fact that I had ruined what could have been quite a good painting (if I may say so myself) by trying to turn it into 'modern art' with lumpy, thick black lettering. To my surprise I received hundreds of DMs and it created a conversation, prompting a day-long dialogue where I reshared the more hilarious messages from my inbox. It was like we were part of one long-standing private joke. I painted more, creating more 'ruined' works, enjoying the back and forth that ensued, motivated by the positive responses and light humour this was generating during an immensely difficult and dull period. 'DO NOT WRITE OVER THIS ONE', 'How are you going to ruin it this time?', 'Why haven't you written over it yet?' – the comments flooded in. When that community feeling occurs, it is intoxicating. It is the beautiful side of social media, but it is also often fleeting. I felt useful, inspired and creative for the first time in a long time.

Most influencers, especially on Instagram, build their brand through aspiration, making life look beautiful, enjoyable, Instagrammable. Usually a creator has a niche, whether that's fashion, fitness or food, but what we all have in common is that we are the sole originators of our content. We are photographers, videographers, copywriters, directors, editors, models and marketing team all rolled into one; creators of independent online magazines, updated daily and evergreen. Some people do outsource once they're big enough, hiring photographers for content days or editors for their YouTube videos, but those of us sat firmly in the middle in terms of audience size usually do everything ourselves and we learn on the job.

Whether or not content is an advert, it is work. If influencers posted nothing in between adverts there would be no adverts at all. Brands are buying advertising space within an already existing cosmos. The unpaid content is what begets the paid content and whilst the sums people are paid for one post may seem eyewatering, the way we are paid is lumpy, irregular and unreliable. As the viral tweet from @davygreenberg goes, 'If I do a job in thirty minutes it's because I spent ten years learning how to do that in thirty minutes. You owe me for the years, not the minutes.' Not every influencer has ten years' experience behind them, but almost every single one has a healthy amount of unpaid content that would have cost them in both time and money, and that somewhat risky investment is what *might* eventually make them valuable to brands. They have built a loyal following among a specific demographic in a way that brands and marketeers have strived to do for years. If you hire a billboard at Twickenham Stadium it will cost you a hell of a lot and will be seen by some sixty thousand sports fans, but, even then, it will be far less targeted than if you hire an influencer. With influencers, perhaps the quote can be rephrased to, 'If I'm paid a thousand pounds for a piece of content, it's because I've amassed a captivated audience through my organic content. I'm being paid for access to my followers, not for the time it took to take the photo.'

Olivia Yallop notes, in her book *Break the Internet*, 'There is a considerable class of creators who aren't making headlines, but who are plugging away at moderately successful content, making a full-time living off monetising their lifestyles and identities.' As we would say on the internet: it me. This is my reality. I am on the inside looking out. Even when I am not thinking about my page in terms of work, I wake up in the morning and consider which parts of my day I will share. Perhaps I'll take a selfie in the gym. Maybe I'll put together an outfit knowing that more than my local barista is going to see it. Maybe it's time to let my followers in on my favourite Sunday roast spot . . . (Actually, this is never happening again, not after Donutgate, when I told people where in South London I got my favourite Nutella-filled donuts and then couldn't get one because they were always sold out.)

It is these individual touches, the humanity and 'relatability' of influencers, that make our pages unlike any other advertising space. But that's where it can get messy. You have to know where to draw the line. When I first started out, I felt a duty to reply to every DM I received, doling out advice late into the night, acting as a proverbial shoulder to cry on for women who looked up to me. While some people hate influencers, many 'users' of social media – a phrase that was forensically dissected in the hit Netflix documentary *Social Dilemma*, which points out that it depicts people on social media as though they were drug addicts, which maybe isn't totally incorrect – adore them and forge para-social relationships with them. These people depend on the creators and their content as a source of comfort, emotional support and community.

As much as this can feel like a great honour, it is also a huge responsibility and you must know your limits. After a while, I realised that not only was this level of support becoming draining, but I wasn't qualified to give it, either. The people seeking my help were often in desperate positions, struggling with their mental health or body image and food-related issues. I was in my early twenties and offering counsel to women often much older than me, naïvely thinking I could help. It shines a light on how many people in our society are unable to access services that could support them. It also demonstrates just how deep the trust runs between influencers and their audiences. It's like the hairdresser who knows the secrets of all of their clients, the softly spoken English teacher who acts as a substitute therapist for troubled students or the Catholic priest who takes confession.

Newton's third law states that, 'For every action in nature, there is an equal and opposite reaction.' Influencers are revered and adored and hated and admonished in equal measure. The conundrum of influencing is that, unlike the influential celebrities of the past – royalty, socialites, actors, models or anyone else who might be

featured in the glossies or tabloids – the public is introduced to us on our way up, rather than once we've
already 'made it'. The appeal of influencers used to be
that you met them whilst they were at university or living on a budget or otherwise giving 'girl-next-door'
energy; we seem to be just like you. I am one of the lucky
ones. When I first started my account it was like TikTok
in terms of being able to go viral and grow your account
quickly. My content was consistently reaching new eye-
balls. There was no pathway, no definitive endgame to
aspire to, no blueprint for success that could act as a
guide.

This is very much unlike today, when recent research
found that one in five British children want a career as
a social media influencer (it was a poll carried out by a
marketing consultancy, but even so). It is a much trick-
ier and more competitive terrain for new creators now,
and I have had the same undulating follower count for
almost four years, sometimes increasing, sometimes
decreasing, but never stagnant. As I get older or make
lifestyle changes my audience ebbs and flows as I
become more or less relatable, interesting or relevant to
them. I used to be obsessed with the numbers, but I
have found that I am in quite a sweet spot. I can make
a living from doing something I love, whilst not being
subject to too much recognition or too much scrutiny.
But the scrutiny is always there.

To refer back to Jack Johnson as I truly am a stan,
he has a song called 'Wasting Time', in which he laments

the fact that everyone walks around thinking that 'everybody knows about everybody else', but they spend so much time preoccupied with these assumptions that they never turn the line of questioning inward and ultimately never get to know themselves. That is sort of what social media is. Or what it can be: a game of ego, insecurity and pseudo-reality.

I feel like I *finally* know myself well, but I have also learnt to accept that over a hundred thousand people might also think they know me pretty well. And there's no way in hell they've got it completely right, because no matter how authentic you think you are online, no matter how much of your 'true self' you try to show, between an organic thought being birthed in your brain and that thought making its way on to a monitored app, there will have been a lot of both subconscious and conscious editing. Whether it be self-censorship for the good of others or little white lies to make yourself look better, no one is truly truthful all the time. This is the same offline, of course, but a conversation in a coffee shop hangs only in the unreliable memories of the people sipping on their oat milk flat whites as they discuss the problem with modern day feminism.

Online, text is free from tone of voice, nuance and context, and every reader infers their own meaning. Are we equipped to take in this much information without all that nuance? Can the human brain contain so many opinions from so many people that we, when it comes down it, don't really know but are inclined to trust and admire because of their social (media) status? When someone makes what is perceived as an off-colour comment, a mob can descend like a swarm of wasps whose nest has been disturbed. Whether the person is a Nazi sympathiser or simply mentioned that they used a different type of bottle to feed their newborn, the ferocity of the swarm is the same. Outrage online respects no middle ground; it is only concerned with stinging the perpetrator and stamping out the wrongdoing, no matter how insignificant that wrongdoing may be in the grand scheme of things. On the flip side, we are tribal beings and mob mentality also means we find solace and comfort on well-trodden paths or, more plainly, we trust people who already have followers. However, when an account gets 'too many' followers, our distrust begins to rise and emulate the way we may feel about a very small account that isn't yet established. Being too established can also be a bad thing.

Interestingly, it is women who mostly dominate these online spaces, expertly and to great commercial end, yet they are not held up as business tycoons, masters of the economy or new age entrepreneurs. To be an influencer is often seen to the uninitiated as an icky, embarrassing thing. Something to be ashamed of. Something to judge. In fact, many see influencers as nothing more than airheads and it can be quite draining to show up every day, especially when that opens you up to all sorts of judgements about everything from the way you look to how you dress and what you eat for your dinner. My trolls have told me I love myself too much and am too obsessed with my looks, but at the same time they've called me unattractive, ugly or a 'butterface'. I didn't know what that meant until my twenty-sixth birthday, when I came across an old gossip website that spelt it out for me: 'Oenone's hot, *but her face.*' I scrutinised the story I had just posted of my birthday outfit, and then went into my camera roll and zoomed in on my face. I examined all the ways I could improve myself: a slimmer nose, fuller lips, a more defined jawline, straighter teeth. Then I went out for dinner with Z and spent the whole meal wondering whether he, too, saw these flaws that I had missed until now. Often influencers are blamed for the rise in certain plastic surgeries, or aesthetics, but frequently they are just conforming to the pressures of their audiences, peers and haters, as much as their followers are influenced by them.

It's so much worse for younger influencers. Take Emma Chamberlain, for example. She was a YouTuber known for her humour and 'likeability', an oddly ephemeral metric, whose fans have grown up with her and feel extremely close to her. I don't watch YouTube very often and came to her late, but one sleepless night I fell down a rabbit hole of her videos. Her whole back catalogue was there for me to binge on and I watched her life change materially in a way that felt intoxicatingly fast. Very rapidly she went from being a fairly normal, young, fun, and quirky sixteen-year-old girl to a very rich, independent not-a girl-not-yet-a-woman living in a vast apartment by herself, but her content also continued to escalate as she grappled with the intensity of having built such a vast, loyal fanbase. In one meta video from 2018, when she was just seventeen, titled 'Why I don't upload that much', she breaks the fourth wall and creates a Sundance-worthy edit of what it takes to be a YouTuber. Her narration starts off as positive and sharply nosedives into a pressure-induced anxiety nightmare. I felt panic just watching it, as well as a huge sense of sadness at the intensity of the stress she was burdened with, yet I was also in awe of her ability to create, her self-awareness and her temerity at such a young age. At one point in the voiceover, she says, 'It's getting quite dark, but it's not that deep, I promise.'

After watching the video, out of curiosity I migrated to the comments (of which there are now almost thirty-thousand) and found myself fascinated by the level of familiarity her audience felt for her, as well as some of the audaciousness from fans who felt let down at her not posting. It's not something I am familiar with; compared to Emma there is a palpable distance between me and my audience. Whilst it was worrying to imagine someone so young feeling responsible for hundreds of thousands of faceless internet users, that same Emma Chamberlain went on to present on the red carpet at the 2022 Met Gala, adorned in diamonds and receiving compliments from mega-model-nepo-babies such as

Hailey Bieber and Gigi Hadid. Her house was recently profiled in *Architectural Digest* and even I couldn't finish the article, as it made me feel so inferior and even jealous. If someone came to know her through this, it may seem as though she's the luckiest twenty-one-year-old on earth, but I certainly couldn't put myself through what she did to get there. Hours of unrelenting work, often met with possessive, obsessive and intrusive commentary that only encouraged her to try harder for an ever-growing army of hungry fans – it may not be working on the frontline, but it's a far cry from the overnight success people attribute to influencers and content creators.

Then again, being an influencer can be hugely lucrative, creatively stimulating and personally rewarding. Admittedly, even sometimes *I* think my job is a bit of a joke. When I snooze my alarm mid-week, unconstrained by the shackles of a corporate nine-to-five, I marvel at the genuine luxury of my lifestyle – not necessarily luxury in the material sense, but in the freedom and autonomy I have to structure my day to day. How the fuck did I get so lucky? Why can't we all live like this? This is often accompanied by a pang of guilt, because what I do know is, perhaps more than any other 'creative' role we have seen before (I'm using quotation marks here as I know some people don't consider it creative), influencing throws the disparity in wealth in the world into harsh relief. It is the abject showiness of the industry that makes it both profitable and distasteful.

Marketing in the US may embrace corny obvious-ness and commercial banality, but in the UK we value a more subtle approach. We do not, as a nation, like being sold to and part of the mystique that the adver-tising industry has previously tried to maintain has been done away with by influencers holding up prod-ucts such as whitening toothpaste next to their neon gnashers, with discount codes and copy-and-paste cap-tions. There is a huge tug of war between creator and consumer, in that many people love to follow the lives of people who profit from being influencers, but once those influencers move away from the lifestyle that made them relatable, the audience can begin to feel dis-illusioned. Was this just about marketing all along? Is this person really my online 'friend'? Or are they just there to get their five minutes of fame and get out?

This is a reasonable accusation, but at the same time a lot of the criticism comes from people who think it's simple, because it is such unknown territory. They believe that anyone can do it, you just need a tripod, a phone and some good lighting (my preference is soft natural light – try sitting in front of a window). But no matter how good you get at lighting and angles, it's almost impossible to grow a profile out of nothing, overnight, which leads me on to the number one ques-tion people have about women of the internet: what do they do all day? Well, pretty much everything we do becomes work. Most people only think about the min-ute it takes to upload an ad and believe shooting ad content must be a quick process. In fact, it usually takes days or more to get an ad copywritten, fully shot and edited. Even if it is just a photo and some stories, it's a much lengthier process than you might imagine. You receive a full brief from the brand, which is usually pretty prescriptive, along with contracts, dos and don'ts, and an entitlement on their side to reshoots. This means that even once you've done the content, you must send it off for approval, after which they could say it's not quite right and ask you to retake it. And after all that, if they still don't like it, or you're not happy, the campaign can be pulled completely.

This happens more than you might think, which means – if you haven't got various streams of revenue – losing out on a pay cheque you were relying on. But fundamentally, it is getting to the point of having a monetizable platform, and sustaining it, that's tricky. Again, it's not rocket science, but it is also not as simple as it seems. If someone said they were a social media manager for a brand, or a content creator for an organisation, or a copywriter, model, photographer, stylist or any number of roles that largely resemble the work an influencer does day to day, many people would readily accept that as a credible career. But there is a huge resistance to believing that what influencers do is actually work. Then again, that's sort of the magic: we're supposed to make it look effortless.

The maintenance of our very being – our appearance, hobbies, friendships, relationships – becomes blurrily intertwined and enmeshed with our 'work'. Unless you set up boundaries, that is. My latest boundary, from my experience with Z, is relationships: the jury is out on whether or not I would ever share my partner on social media, but I have made a firm decision that I would never share any potential future children's faces – perhaps the backs of their heads à la Blake Lively, Fearne Cotton and Angela Scanlon. However, for those people who built a following as a family account, or as a mummy blogger, it is almost impossible to go back without risking your entire livelihood. Good, some may say, your children shouldn't be used for profit, but once you have entangled that much of yourself and your life with your work, it can be tricky to go back without huge repercussions. It can be difficult to see an alternative path.

As I grow up with my platform, I crave ever more privacy. Not just because of the fear of people having too much access to me, but because I am also slowly trying to figure out what drives me to do or share things in the first place. If a tree falls in the forest and no one is around to hear it, does it make a sound? If I fall in love again and there aren't photos for my audience to see, does it mean any less? These are the things I was trying to figure out after my break-up with Z, because I had built the beast before I knew what it was or, indeed, who I was.

Chapter 3

IN MY FINAL year at uni, I had a sort of awakening. I found two new love interests: podcasts and Beth. I was spending a lot more time on my own, as most of my closest friends had finished their degrees and left Cardiff for London, where they were starting their big, grown-up jobs. I finally resolved to stop seeking myself in all the wrong places and began to deal with some quite difficult self-reckoning and self-introspection, including, but not limited to, who I was and how I was perceived because of my class status. Having been surrounded by mostly upper-middle class peers from the age of eleven, my attempts to fit in were through Jack Wills tracksuits, Kipling backpacks and Hunter wellies. The realisation that my well-established uniform of pearl stud earrings, fur coats and received pronunciation was more alienating than endearing came much too late in my opinion. A middle-class upbringing can also incubate a belief that the world is fair and everyone is afforded the same opportunities as you, so much so that you are unable to even recognise those privileges.

I was desperate to be liked and I wore my loudness like a safety blanket, using it to shield the fragility I felt inside, but as my introspection began to turn itself outward I sensed that what at school was frequently called my 'gift of the gab' was sometimes perceived as arrogance or interrogation. I became more self-conscious, not of how I looked, but of who I was. It was, at this stage, only a low-level hum, a niggling suspicion that somewhere during my twenty years I had missed something and that it was visible to everyone except me. Simultaneously, I became aware of the fact that I had been sleeping on my intelligence. More than that, actively burying it. Despite having always liked to be teacher's pet – I was an absolute *pick me*, whatever the setting – I preferred to play the dumb blonde outside the classroom and never really pushed myself intellectually. I'd never really had to. In your teenage years it feels as though the world is happening to you. Every bad grade, every break-up, every argument with a parent is simply a consequence of the world you've been brought into, through no doing or asking of your own. Whilst you may accept responsibility for kicking your friend under the table, farting during assembly or not doing your homework, conceptualising that any deeper ripple effect could ricochet into the universe without your consent, simply by virtue of your existence, is near impossible. Or, at least, it was for me.

I started paying more attention to books and became a voracious reader. I had always been a bookworm as a child and I had to read for university, of course, but for the first time I became almost evangelical about what books could *teach us*, rather than just seeing them as a pleasurable hobby or form of escapism. I had also become obsessed with podcasts. They did for me what years of lectures from parents and literal lectures never could: they made learning interesting and fundamentally cool. I decided to share with my followers what I was learning. *The Guilty Feminist* and *The High Low* were my soundtrack from the end of 2016 until *The High Low* ended in 2020. I still love *The Guilty Feminist*. Those two podcasts, in particular, were my gateway drug into feminism. Despite studying feminist modules at university, it was having these women in my ears that really sparked something in me. There was something about the medium of audio, coupled with women taking charge of the narrative and the angle of the conversation that absolutely revolutionised my thinking. They were engaging, bright and literary, but never out of touch. I never felt locked out of the conversation as I had done with some of the male-led podcasts I had tried to listen to previously. They felt welcoming, as though they were designed for me, and I was learning. I couldn't believe that I hadn't realised all the things at play all around me, all the time. I began to question myself, my motives, my beliefs. *The Guilty Feminist*'s Deborah Frances-White often joked that she had left one cult (the Jehovah's Witnesses), only to form another, and I was a willing and ready member. I was obsessed with her podcast; with her.

Influencers are so involved with image, with visuals, and podcasters aren't, but the experience of being a podcaster is fundamentally very similar: people build an audience and create revenue through advertising products to their loyal followers. However, unlike the female influencers I looked up to on image-sharing platforms, who prioritised their appearance, these women were championing their ideas, opinions and expertise. The seed for my own podcast, *Adulting*, was being planted, but it was still a while off yet.

My new friendship with Beth also nourished a part of me that I had neglected for far too long. I spent hours sitting cross-legged on her kitchen windowsill, drinking red wine and smoking rollies, as Beth exasperatedly tried to explain Thatcherism and neo-liberalism to me, for the third time. A group of us stayed up all night watching the 2016 US elections, with Beth acting as our translator, answering our questions about what was unfolding and why it was happening. Of course, that summer Britain had also voted to leave the EU. A lot of shit went down in 2016, so perhaps my political awakening really taking hold when it did wasn't surprising.

I still had a lot to learn and now I can see that I made

some downright embarrassing mistakes. Everything I posted soon became portrayed in an entirely misguided feminist light. On International Women's Day I posted a headless, topless selfie with an earnest, and what I thought to be, feminist message. I was wearing high-waisted H&M jeans, a contrived smile and nothing else. I had covered my boobs with my forearm and sort of squished them against me, which made them look fake. The caption was about freeing the nipple. I felt like it was important, shocking or at least game-changing. At the time it made me feel empowered, that I was breaking the rules, being subversive, but as far as actual feminism goes it did nothing. I obviously must have realised this, as I deleted it soon after.

But misguided or not, I became more vocal and emboldened. I would lament the sexualisation of female fitness Instagrammers on my story and write blog posts about the inaccessibility of gyms for women. I even emailed *The Guilty Feminist* asking them to cover the topic of women feeling like they weren't welcome in the gym. These little introductions to feminism may seem arbitrary or even self-serving, but they got me engaged, they piqued my interest and started me on a quest to learn more about the world, how I fitted into it and, by extension, how my identity as a fitness Instagrammer fitted into that. There was a lot to be grappling with, in that respect. My male flatmates would constantly question how what I was doing was feminist, as I spent hours locked away in my bedroom, attempting to get the perfect booty shot to accompany my heartfelt prose about finally finding peace with my body. I would rather leak my notes in my iPhone app (something which I would never, ever, want to do), than have had a spy camera in my university rooms throughout my fitness influencing era. The grunts, sighs, huge exhalations and breathing exercises I would endure to get the perfect mirror selfie . . . horrifying. I was literally studying the suffragettes for my degree and yet I somehow still managed to believe that my biggest fight was making sure I was allowed to show my Primark-thonged butt online.

At the same time, as I became more comfortable being viewed as an authority on fitness, I truly started to feel the weight of my following. It had now grown to ten thousand and, coming from a family of doctors who want empirical evidence for *literally everything*, I decided I needed to be accountable if I was going to keep on talking about fitness online. I also began to wonder if I could genuinely have a career as a PT. Even if it was just a side hustle to sustain me for a while, I figured my following would be a useful tool for gaining clients. After researching the different courses to qualify as one, it became obvious that I couldn't afford them. Emily, always generous, said she would take out a loan and lend me the money, and I could pay her back incrementally from the income I was sure I'd make doing online coaching. I gratefully accepted her offer.

It wasn't until I qualified later that summer that I started to hear whispers of the word influencer and that some girls in London were being paid to advertise products on their Instagram. Back then, the Advertising Standards Agency (ASA) had not stepped in to regulate sponsored content online. There was a period when it just sort of looked like product placement, so followers didn't know what content was paid for and what wasn't. I found out that if you had a medium-sized following, the more products you featured, the more likely it was you would get noticed by the brands, so it was commonplace to spend hours creating unpaid content that *looked* like ad content. Even when we didn't realise people were getting paid for their posts, we would create product-led content. We just thought it was the 'done thing' to grow our accounts.

We would feature products that were relevant to what we were posting about, from blog post reviews of protein powders, photos of us in our favourite leggings with a long-winded caption about how soft they were, or a new recipe for zoats (that's zucchini oats, if you don't know, don't worry, it was bad times) using a fancy peanut butter. I decided to hold a '10k giveaway', unaware that this was often used as a marketing tool, not a 'giving back to my followers to say thanks' tool. I reached out to brands for gifting and to my surprise they were more than willing to supply products. Although I am sure many people do hold giveaways out of kindness or reciprocity, as I did, they also have a great commercial benefit, especially for the brand. The idea is that people tag each other under the post to win and follow the influencer as well as the brand in order to be entered into the draw, thus driving engagement and followers for both parties. My giveaway included sachets of protein powder, Frylight (a one-calorie oil spray for cooking) and various other diet-focussed products.

As my Instagram friends and I all started to wise up to the fact that we were building something valuable and had bargaining power, we began to share business tips and ideas, supporting each other's content online and making sure we interacted whenever we posted anything. We noticed that once one person commented it would encourage more engagement, but, more truthfully, we did it because we found it embarrassing and exposing if our words and pictures hung suspended on our page to no response. Nowadays this is called a 'pod' and it's not strictly legal, as you sort of inorganically hack the system. I often get DMs asking if I want to be added to thousand-strong 'pods', the members of which all engage with each other's content to boost that content up the algorithm. There were only ten to fifteen of us doing it in our group, and we were genuinely supporting each other and it was never dishonest, but it's funny just how much we managed to get right without knowing it at the time. The more hours we were plugging in, uploading in real time, reacting, creating and sharing, the more we were rewarded. I was gaining around five thousand new followers each month, and sometimes more in one go after a particularly successful post. It wasn't just my

Instagram peers and follower growth that felt exciting, but the fact that I had access to these women that I was engaging with day to day through my content.

Meanwhile, my conversations with Beth were becoming less random and more frequent. We were initially on opposite sides of the debate, but soon my calculated dumb-blonde persona – a persona I had been so fond of, so protected by – started to feel really uncomfortable, like an itchy Halloween wig you can't wait to take off. My feminism had thus far only concerned itself with whether or not I should be able to post sexually liberated content online (read: I wanted to post belfies without being slut-shamed), but Beth would challenge why I even wanted to dress a certain way in the first place. I remember one rather heated conversation outside a sandwich shop where she repeatedly asked me who I dressed for, almost reducing me to tears as she introduced me to the concept of self-objectification. She actually rendered me speechless for the first time in a long time as I realised that I didn't know what I thought about anything, only what I had been conditioned to believe. From then on, I went to Beth for advice on absolutely everything. The antithesis of the women I followed online, she was my own feminist encyclopedia and exactly how you'd imagine her, always wearing an unravelling cardigan, with a packet of baccy sticking out of her pocket. She had a joyful lack of concern about her appearance and a personal vendetta against make-up. She is beautiful, by the way, but for her this was inconsequential. I felt so torn between the two worlds; like I had to choose; like I couldn't be both.

When I finally graduated in the summer of 2017 I was ready for a new chapter. My university experience had been a weird one, all in all. I had felt out of place, never quite finding my groove, flitting between groups, jobs and identities. The only steadfast part had been my Instagram.

Poppie, Yas, Steph and I went on a girls' holiday to Spain, where we lamented being the oldest on the Fuengirola strip, while fending off teenage boys who would try to snog us when we went out at night. I carried on posting workouts from the sweaty little resort gym and more bikini pictures than were warranted, really.

Upon my return, my parents were keen for me to finally figure out what I was going to do for a living, as being a PT didn't seem viable to them given the min-imal income I was making from my coaching. I planned to live at home until I secured a job and could follow my friends and make the pilgrimage to London. With my parents living in the middle of nowhere and me not having yet (or to date) passed my driving test, I was relying on their generosity to drive me to the gym while I was under their roof. One day, my dad dropped me off and I sauntered into the gym in my pastel green Nike Metcons, clutching my over-ear headphones and Canon G7M11, feeling like quite the professional.

I had been working on my box jumps when it

happened, but foolishly, in order to get higher, I had turned one of the brightly coloured cubes on its side, rather than adding another block on top and securing it with Velcro. As I landed, the box slid from under me and I fell to the sound of a crack. More flushed with embarrassment than any pain, I looked around me for any witnesses and was relieved that no one seemed to have been paying me any attention. I saw my headphones on the floor next to me and assumed the worrying noise had come from the impact as they hit the ground. I went to stand up. As I did, my leg gave way. 'Fuck,' I thought to myself. No stranger to injury, I assumed it was a sprain. Once I'd hoisted myself up, I attempted to walk. The pain was agony. I waved sheepishly at two personal trainers, who carried me over to the sofa, where I lifted my ankle and rang my dad. While waiting for him, I opened my vlogging camera. I watched back the footage of my fall. Sure enough, it was all captured, along with unmistakeable evidence that the crack I had heard seemed to be coming from my ankle, rather than my Beats by Dre. Sure enough, by the time my dad picked me up, my ankle was the size of a tennis ball and throbbing, and shortly after arriving at A&E I was informed that it was broken.

This should have been a massive setback. Oddly, for both my work and content it proved to be one of my most fruitful periods. I gained more followers over that six-week period of convalescence than I ever have before or since. I was stuck at home with my leg in a boot, non-weight bearing, and mildly delirious from all the painkillers. The mixture of happy inebriation and the sheer boredom of being sequestered in Somerset and unable to move meant I engaged with my audience the most I ever had. Which is saying a lot. I would wake up early in the morning to document my recovery, having christened my injured leg Sally, and personifying her further by giving her an Australian accent. I would post about Sally wasting away, attempting to do one-legged yoga and upper body workouts, while ensuring I was still sharing useful fitness-related information. I chatted away to my followers all day long and my engagement soared. I was so grateful for my online community; it made what could have been a really depressing time a lovely one.

Now I was missing Beth, who was swanning off around the globe, I started talking to my audience about the things I used to discuss with her. Then I had an idea. Communicating online was great, but it wasn't the same as really getting into it in person. I created a Facebook group for a book club and shared the link with my followers. I wrote that I was seeking a seminar-style discussion centred on a book, but not limited to just that. So many answered positively that a few weeks later my mum and I drove to London to meet the fifty or so women who had put five pounds each into a kitty for food and drink, for the first of what would end up being my now sell-out monthly events. The first book we read was *Hot Mess* by Lucy Vine, which I had gobbled up by the pool on my girls' holiday in Spain. I had adored it because I completely related to it, feeling like a hot mess too with all my heartbreaks. In the back of an old, unassuming pub in Kennington, our group discussed relationships, feminism and what it meant to be a woman. I got back home to Somerset full of hope and excitement. I was realising that there were so many opportunities that came with having a following, not just potential brand deals, but also access to like-minded women, who like me were traversing their twenties, eager to learn more about the world and themselves.

Declaring yourself a feminist became a rite of passage. The movement was having a mainstream resurgence and a lot of it was happening on social media. Like me, many others enjoyed learning in a more accessible way about concepts that had previously felt very academic or even extreme. There had been a time when my perception of a feminist was a man-hating, hairy-armpitted, Mooncup-wearing weirdo. Save for the man-hating part, I don't see any of those things as weird now. I learned to love a Mooncup (I have since graduated to period pants – the best, if you ask me), tested out hair growth and announced myself as a feminist with pleasure. Whenever I put up a question box for my audience to ask me anything, the questions became more skewed towards social justice issues, objectification and the patriarchy than how to slow boil an egg or get abs. I can remember feeling a surge of pride when a fellow fitness influencer tagged me in a story that asked: 'How come

Oenone gets such interesting questions and everyone just asks me about weightloss?' I would mostly keep my feed posts to fitness or food-related content, but on my stories I'd share resources, articles or podcasts that had taught me something new.

This was a post I sent out in September 2017 – the text was on a pink background:

'They say that I look like a boy, or I am too masculine, too many opinions, my body is too strong. So, baby, girl we don't change. We take the gravel and the shell and we make a pearl. And we help other people to change so that they can see more kinds of beauty.'

Caption: I absolutely loved @pink's speech at the VMAs. I thought it was so poignant. There is beauty in diversity and ofc in kindness. Happy Saturday #TheTinyTank

This was the era of Sheryl Sandberg's *Lean In* feminism, when 'girlboss' was used in earnest rather than in the current formulation of 'Gaslight, gatekeep, girlboss'. My audience and I were mainly white, middle-class women, completely swept up in the undoing of our reverence for men, and our criticism of the patriarchy and all the ways in which it oppressed us. At this point we hadn't yet acknowledged how complicit we were in the oppression and marginalisation of so many others, but we were some of the loudest voices in a fight that we had only just joined and knew very little about. Not necessarily me personally at this point, but women who looked and sounded like me. Whilst on the one hand, this mass uptake in this new wave of feminism was revolutionary, on the other it was delivered in a soft hue of millennial pink and ultimately yassified (internet slang originating from the Black queer community which, according to Wiktionary, means, 'The act of applying several beauty filters to a picture using a photo-editing application such as FaceApp until the subject becomes almost unrecognizable.').

It was useful, though, for a time. We talked about periods brazenly, shook off shame about masturbation and ultimately allowed ourselves to embrace everything we had been taught to hide. Once again social media allowed the space for 'non-mainstream' conversations or ideas to become mainstream. To help people see that maybe their views were outdated, it was easy to point them in the direction of posts, podcasts or videos that had already been viewed or liked by thousands of others.

The more I shared what I was learning, the more my page became a safe place for debate and constructive criticism. My audience would pull me up when my opinion was problematic or when I had misunderstood something. I welcomed their feedback. My page became a two-way street. I shared my knowledge on fitness and what I had learnt, and in return my audience started to teach me about myself. As this was my ever-ongoing quest, I was ready to learn.

Over the next few years, I did exactly that. I immersed myself further in podcasts, books, articles and documentaries. I learnt about privilege, intersectional feminism, politics and identity politics. Like the rest of my generation, it seemed, I had 'woken' up. In 2018 I launched my podcast, *Adulting*. I interviewed guests such as Doris and Valerie, two women who I was introduced to through the charity Choose Love, who had fled Cameroon as refugees due to their sexuality, and Kojo Apeagyei, a poet, writer and social activist who worked at the charity, Shelter, after being homeless for a time. I interviewed Bruce and Kelsey, who ran a viral Instagram account called @nowhitesaviours, about structural racism and what white saviourism actually is, and Cambell Kenneford, a trans model and influencer who had appeared on a Channel 4 show called *Gender Quake*. I spoke to politicians, activists, athletes, journalists, doctors, influencers, authors and everyone in between. We explored gender, sexuality, race, culture, relationships, money and what it means to be human. I did all of this out of a genuine belief that if I was to have a platform, as a white, cis-het, privately educated, able-bodied woman – all labels that shaped how I saw the world and how the world saw me – then I needed to make sure that the conversations I was having spoke to more than my limited, privileged experiences.

At the time, in 2018, this felt organic, genuine and, hopefully, in some way helpful and useful. As time went on, and when I eventually decided to stop the podcast, it was because suddenly it started to feel contrived. I was worried about my position, as a person of so much privilege, hosting these conversations. I started to question whether I had got it all wrong even venturing into this arena in the first place. And because I couldn't be sure that I was the right person to be holding the mic, after a hundred and three episodes, in July 2021, I released my last. This was exactly what had happened with fitness, although I hadn't started to see the pattern yet. It was the Dunning-Kruger effect, a cognitive bias in which people over-estimate their own abilities. When I started to learn about something new there was so much to share with my followers, but as soon as I thought I had reached the precipice, the fog would clear and I would realise I was still at the bottom of the mountain. It was always at this point that I stepped back, knowing that in order to become an actual expert I would need to dedicate my life and my work to that one thing. I would need to go away and study, and gain ten thousand hours of experience. I could do those things, but not with the world watching.

Similarly, in 2020, when the news of the murder of George Floyd started circulating on Twitter, as we were all confined to our homes and glued to our screens, so many people, including me, felt so much anger and distress that we felt we needed to, in some way, try to change this systematically unjust world. I don't know how to write about this, not in any specific, meaningful way, not without centring myself. At the time what I did felt right, but I don't know now if I should've been so vocal. I was so genuinely passionate and furious and eager to help in any way I could. It felt like all those years of learning were crucial evidence that I must use my voice and platform, to show others in my position how and why we, too, were the problem.

In *Get Rich or Lie Trying*, Symeon Brown writes about the ever-growing activist-to-influencer/entrepreneur pipeline. Activism, or clicktivism as it is sometimes called, has now become a form of brand-building in and of itself. We learnt to speak the language of activism in tandem with consumption. Swipe up to sign a petition/email your local MP, and then swipe up to buy my jumper. Whether the account is a faceless hub of infographics and content repurposed into digestible bites or an individual with a cause, the lines of altruism become heavily blurred once digitised sharing gets involved. It used to be seen as uncouth to share a good deed. If you gave money to the homeless, gave up your seat on the bus, or gave an arm to an old lady to help her across the road, you wouldn't necessarily go home and tell everyone about it. It was understood that we should be doing those things out of good will, rather than self-gratification, but we have seen how the power of social media can move mountains for social causes, so many of us decided that sharing good deeds was no longer about ego but about the greater good. There's a difference between being on the frontline of any movement and spearheading change higher up. Both, it became apparent, are powerful, but they are different.

Activism online doesn't require your audience to have the budget for designer handbags or beautiful holidays, like some traditional content. You can, or could, grow relatively quickly by creating content that pulls people to share it, things you feel like you can't just scroll past. '10 things you should know about BLM', 'What no one has told you about Yemen', 'Iran needs you' – these posts tug on our heart strings and consciences, and we feel compelled to share them, even if it's just so we can feel good for having done so. I started to share fewer resources as I started to realise everyone I followed was posting the same infographics. Is this helpful? I wondered. Do my followers need me to post something that everyone else has shared or am I posting it to show that I am aware, that I am not ignorant?

Again, I started to cordon off parts of myself. I did my learning in private. I wanted to know that I was genuinely engaging with something for me or for the cause, rather than clout. Once again, I found myself feeling a discord with the content I was putting out. Where *Adulting* had felt like a genuine investigation into the culture we live in, it started to feel like I was inadvertently feeding the culture wars narrative. I was worried that I was setting myself up for a fall. Then again, my last actual fall, the one that resulted in my broken ankle, had turned out not to be such a bad thing. In the long term that fracture created time for me to reflect and open my mind to the world. Maybe this was going to be alright, too?

Chapter 4

IN MY LAST year of uni I had secured one paid advertisement on my Instagram for a food-tracking app for a staggering five hundred pounds. In exchange I shared how the app worked: it provided recipes that encouraged its users to seek out healthier meal choices and learn more about the macro-nutrient properties of foods. In the caption I declared it was an advert, even though there was no regulation that said I had to. I felt nervous about it, but five hundred pounds was an unfathomable amount of money to me and I couldn't quite believe it had happened.

So when I hit seventy thousand followers in the aftermath of my broken ankle, I began to wonder if maybe I was on to something, for real this time. My friend, now an established influencer, who had started to make good, *real* money from her Instagram, told me that her sister – who had a much smaller following – had just signed with a new agency. Perhaps they might sign me too? I called them and was invited to come into their office in Soho for a meeting to discuss what my plans were for the future and whether we would be a good fit for each other. They also said, in no uncertain terms, that with my following I needn't look for any other jobs. Should they take me on, as a minimum I would be making £2,000 a month from ads. If I hadn't already been sitting down, that would've knocked me over. My laptop had so many job application tabs open for various advertising agencies, magazines and graduate schemes, it was burning my lap through my dressing gown.

I told my parents straight away. After five minutes of uninterrupted gabble I took a deep breath. They were immediately sceptical and slightly exasperated. I could see from the looks on their faces they were thinking, 'When will she just grow up and get a real job?' Not having considered such things as taxes or transportation or the general cost of living in London, I told them it would be enough money to live off. They were eventually, and as ever, supportive; more so after seeing the look of desperation on my face when I dropped a dollop of frozen yoghurt that I was eating directly out of the tub on to my black moon boot. They agreed that one of them would drive me to London for this 'interview', but if it didn't work out I really did need to figure out what I was doing – and ASAP. As a first job, it was to me the absolute dream. I couldn't believe it. I just wanted to support myself and buy some time whilst I figured out what I was going to do when I grew up, eventually.

I was still using crutches when I was dropped off in Soho on a September afternoon. I wore Topshop pleather Joni jeans (RIP), a long-sleeved tie top that was my mum's from the 80s and I completed the look with *one* of her statement Russell and Bromley boots on one foot and my ginormous protective moon boot on the other. The late-teen balmy weather, mixed with the fake leather, boots and crutches, meant that when I arrived at the offices I looked like Kate Moss in that scene in the *Absolutely Fabulous* movie when she walks out of the Thames. I was soaked with sweat. This doesn't happen to me so much anymore, but when I was younger, if I was nervous, I would give Lee Evans a run for his money.

The office was the epitome of late-2010s start-up cool, all wood and copper pipes, exposed bricks and Rubik's cubes. The open-plan basement was populated by a few young and attractive employees working on MacBooks. The founder was floppy-haired, softly spoken and not very old for someone so senior. In fact, he was roughly the same age as me, but I felt infantilised in his presence and intimidated by all his business acumen (which I had inferred from the fact that he ran a business with a cool office in Soho). He told me to make a list of every brand I had ever dreamed of collaborating with and said that by the end of the year it was likely that they would all come to fruition, and then some. I was blown away. It felt too good to be true. He explained to me that the agency's ethos was all about influencers having 'longevity'. They didn't want to cash in on someone's fifteen minutes of fame, but instead turn influencers into businesses and brands in their own right, meaning not only marketing other people's products, but eventually, owning their own. I remember thinking this was groundbreaking at the time and he wasn't wrong. That route is now a well-trodden path for influencers. Think Molly Mae's fake tan, Sarah Ashcroft's clothing label and Deliciously Ella's food range. I was still sweating profusely as I signed my name on the dotted line and smeared foundation across the top of the page from my sleeve, having used it as a makeshift handkerchief.

That evening I went to the pub with some friends and animatedly told them about my interview. They sat there with painted on smiles, trying to look happy for me, but were clearly dubious. Eventually, they confirmed that whilst it was *so exciting*, it did just sound like another of my escapades. They didn't want me to get swept up and be all hopeful and optimistic, when, realistically, how was I going to survive just doing Instagram? 'It's not like a *real job*,' one of them said and for the first couple of years they were right. It was tough to survive in London.

On 14 October 2017 I moved in with my university friend David. We had done a lot of flat-hunting and eventually fell in love with a second-floor flat up Brixton Hill. It was over our monthly budget, but I was desperate for this place. It had bevelling along the ivory walls in the hall, gorgeous bay windows and a huge statement mirror in the lounge. To my twenty-three-year-old eyes it looked like it was straight out of *House & Garden* and had been done by an interior designer. Not only was it homely and cosy, but I also thought it was the perfect setting to take photos. I said I would pay a bit more for the larger room, feeling confident that I would be able to make it work based on that one conversation with my agent and little to no financial literacy.

When I moved in, I was still doing online coaching, but after having paid our hefty deposit and the first month's rent, I didn't really have much in the way of savings and started to worry about how I would pay the next instalment. I was in constant contact with my management, as they advised me on how to make my Instagram more monetisable, and sent me over invitations to events and leads for ad campaigns. However, so far, no suitable paid ads had really come in. A mixture of stupidity, privilege and pure optimism meant that, against everyone's advice, I had faith that this was going to work out, despite all the evidence pointing to the contrary. Everyone, from fledgling influencer friends to my parents, was telling me that maybe it was time I looked for 'a real job' – that phrase again. I think half the reason I was even able to make it in this industry is because I can be quite blasé when it comes to uncertainty and insecurity. I don't mind failure that much – if anything, I almost expect it. What's more, if influencing didn't work out for me, who was going to care? Nobody thought it would anyway. I had a degree, a get-up-and-go attitude and, if it failed, I would just get that 'real job'.

As crunch time approached on my rent payment, my agency sent an email over for an ad for Bingo Bongo, a text service that claims to predict your future. This sort of thing was all the rage when I was at school, much to our parents' chagrin, as the texts would cost you exorbitant amounts. It wasn't exactly the Nike sponsorship I had been hoping for, but it was an unbelievable nine hundred pounds for one post, which was enough to cover my excessively expensive rent. So that first month in London, I paid my rent with the fee from that one ad and hoped the rest would sort itself out (the rest being money for bills and food).

Like some sort of timely angel, a friend of mine told me about an app called Into, which allowed people with Instagram followers to eat in different restaurants, bars and cafes around London for free. The offerings were staggered based on the number of followers you had, so for example where someone with ten thousand followers might be offered a coffee at Grind in exchange for a story, another person with two hundred thousand might be offered a three-course meal at a swanky new restaurant in Chelsea. Every day I ventured into Soho and ate poke bowls or vegan soul bowls or loaded burritos, diligently posting and tagging on my stories #gifted. To all those watching it must've seemed like I was living a life of luxury. In reality, I was too embarrassed to admit that they were often my only sustenance. For my followers and family alike it looked like I had it all sorted out, although I was finally starting to doubt this dream. Maybe it *was* too good to be true. I picked up more online coaching clients and for the following year I mostly supported myself with that. The promise of Nespresso and Adidas ads never materialised.

I wanted to be financially stable and make good choices money-wise, but the truth was I'd always had a complicated relationship with money, although some of my experiences growing up gave me enough insight to understand that my income was precarious and I needed to start making smarter decisions. Growing up in the Lake District my family was very comfortable. We lived in a grand Edwardian house and went to the local state school. My dad drove a brand-new BMW, we went on an annual summer holiday and, really, we wanted for nothing. But when I was seven, my dad lost his job and couldn't find work for a few years, and then came the financial crash, which compounded his money issues. Emily had won a swimming scholarship to Millfield when we still lived in the Lakes, so we eventually moved to Somerset to be nearer to her and the school. My parents decided to send me there from year seven and my eldest sister, Tiffany, from sixth form. However, they weren't really in a financial position to do so. They scrimped, saved and borrowed every penny for our education. Luckily for them, as I was the third child, the school offered a discount – buy two, get twenty-five percent off! Most of the rest of my fees was made up of a bursary and scholarship, but even then it was beyond their means.

When I read Adam Buxton's memoir, *Ramble Book*, I found striking similarities between his dad and mine, particularly their strong belief that a private education was essential for the creation of a well-rounded, decent, intelligent person. I feel so lucky to have gone to a private school, but ideologically it's not a decision I would make for my children, if I ever have any. I thought it was the entire universe when I was there and I was infatuated with the place. But my parents have been in debt for as long as I could remember. I would answer the doorbell to men in long black coats, who would tower above me, asking if my dad was home. As I cowered below them in my dressing gown, I'd see their coats as cloaks and wonder if they were from the Ministry of Magic. They were, in fact, debt collectors.

In my last year of school, like she did for my PT course, Emily took a loan out to pay for my last term. She was a medical student herself at the time. Things are still tight for my parents. Like many people, they've never fully financially recovered from 2008 and my dad, at sixty-six, still works incredibly hard. He drives across the country for hours at a time, staying away from home for days on end, and I have never actually heard him complain once. I have the utmost respect for him and the way he gave us what he believed to be the best start in life, even though it meant a life full of financial uncertainty and stress, and cost him more than just money, because he missed out on most of our childhood, too.

Despite the income being sporadic, it would be remiss of me not to acknowledge just how much fun and how exciting those first six months were. I started to get invited to parties with other influencers and sometimes celebrities. Occasionally, my friends would send screenshots of me in the *Daily Mail* TV & Showbiz section. I was never the intended subject of the photograph, it was more mouth-wide-open-drunkenly-eating-a-burger-behind-Vicky-Pattison sort of vibes. Frequently I would get concerned calls from my mum asking me if I was doing any work or just going to parties. I said the parties were work, which was somewhat true. The entry into this world was fascinating and alluring, and I wanted to experience it all.

I remember one party, in particular, for a fast-fashion brand pop-up in Soho. I was stood in the queue for the loo – glamorous – feeling I was very familiar with the back of the head of the person in front of me. He turned around. It was Ed Westwick. This was prior to the allegations and I was a huge *Gossip Girl* fan. I decided to pretend I had no idea who he was. If I fangirled he'd scarper, I reasoned. My tactic worked. That was until his girlfriend at the time, who I didn't know about, got annoyed at me for talking to him so much and yanked the hood of my red puffa coat I was wearing. I took the hint. Later that evening, I got into an argument with a talent manager who said he was encouraging his young YouTuber to do a twenty-eight-day fast because it was 'getting really good views'. In my young, earnest passion, I told him that this was dangerous and irresponsible. He told me to 'shut up' and that he was the manager of a famous young model (who I shan't name, but you know her), as if that would make me respect him.

I had a lot of experiences like this. I hadn't quite worked out the delicate nature of the industry. There were so many unwritten rules, so many unspoken hierarchies. You're allowed into the restaurant, but there isn't a seat for you at the table. I wasn't there to give my opinion or be myself, but to take and share photos They wanted my reach, not me. It was still intoxicating at first, being in such close proximity to people who had previously felt so far away, but after a while the shine wore off. The parties weren't that great and the only people who stayed very long were the people like me, the ones who couldn't get over the free-flowing booze, food and people-watching. The *actual* celebrities would turn up, looking immaculate and gorgeous, do paparazzi walks outside the venue, follow a courteous loop of the event, dish out some air kisses and then hop off in a cab to their next function or just go home. It's all a mirage, I remember thinking.

In the satirical black comedy *Triangle of Sadness*, there is a scene where an influencer who has been invited on to a luxury cruise has asked her boyfriend to take photos of her posing with a large bowl of spaghetti. When he stops, she takes the phone to look at the photos and simultaneously pushes the bowl away. 'Aren't you going to eat that?' asks a bemused guest sat at their table. She says no, she's allergic. Now, I really *don't* want to make you believe that all influencers are terrible, but I did go to some fitness influencer brunches where girls ordered plates of food, featured the decadent eggs benedict and bacon-laden pancakes in their vlogs, and then left without touching a morsel. I have also been to dinners where not one scrap was left. But, yeah, Ruben Östlund got that part pretty on the money.

I decided to come up with a new strategy. If I didn't have a plus one or know anyone, which was often, rather than try to impose myself on those who saw me as, well, an imposition, I would make a bee-line for the PR. They were always good fun, always ready to enjoy the evening that they had worked so hard to create and fundamentally seemed more normal, as I felt I was. This meant I built strong relationships with various women and men in the industry, who got to know me personally and who would think of me when opportunities arose. I started getting more work this way, rather than through my agents. Like any industry, I imagine, a lot of it is about relationships. Follower count and engagement only go so far, so when there's twenty candidates who fit the profile, it usually comes down to personal preference. Often the PRs who reach out to work with me on a campaign will start the email by saying that they have followed and loved my Instagram for years or are avid listeners of my podcast. Sometimes, a brand that has ghosted me forever will hire a new PR and suddenly I will find myself working with them. I used to imagine that brands would just send over a product and pay the influencer to feature it, but the industry is much more sophisticated than that, particularly now. In July 2022, an article in *Forbes* stated that more than fifty-million people around the world consider themselves to be influencers[3] so, whilst brands might have big budgets for influencer marketing spend, it's not enough for that many people to be getting paid and paid well.

I knew I was bringing in a lot of the work myself, as the PRs were either reaching out to me directly via Instagram or my agents forwarded me emails I knew were the results of conversations I'd had with a PR. Despite this, they wouldn't allow me direct access to the emails that came in for me and I had to have their email address in my bio, so no one was able to get straight to me. It was frustrating as I felt this slowed down the process, as they continued to send me ads for things I would never want to advertise. 'Would you work with this diet brand?' No, I definitely wouldn't. 'We've just got one come in for Dairylea?' I was vegan at the time.

Yes, of course I was a vegan, because this was another phenomenon sweeping a newly engaged generation and we were egging each other on. This wasn't necessarily a

---

[3] 'The Rise Of The Influencer: Predictions For Ways They'll Change The World', Joe Gagliese, *Forbes*, July 2022.

bad thing, but it was the start of more black and white thinking. Suddenly, the online world was not only becoming more socially conscious, but also more polarised and lots of us in our twenties were desperate not to get things wrong. It wasn't good enough to know about climate change, we ought to be acting on it and shaming each other when we slipped up. I was terrified to forget my keep-cup in case someone saw me out with a disposable coffee cup and worried about opening my DMs after being tagged in a story using a straw at a friend's party. We were all trying our best, but we were also condemning each other to failure by having such unattainably high standards.

Because of all this, I was probably the worst client for an agency that was looking for someone who would put their principles to one side. Save for that Bingo Bongo ad, which I did out of total desperation, I felt nervous about making money from my platform. I was ruthless in saying no to work unless it entirely aligned with my beliefs, and I didn't want to do affiliate links because in my mind that was my audience paying me and that made me feel guilty – I wanted the *brands* to pay me. I had learnt so much about privilege and I was trying to reconcile this new information with earning money. It wasn't pure altruism; more youthful naïvety. I felt that if, as people told me, I had been given so much privilege already, I had to be cautious about what I took. That may have come from a good place, but earning money from your work is a necessity. The problem was, despite the hours I invested in growing and maintaining my platform, I still hadn't been registering my 'work' as work. I kept seeing it all as a stroke of luck, similar to my luck of being born in the UK, into comfortable circumstances. My career felt like another unfair advantage. I felt like I had something to prove.

My agents came back to me with another idea: to launch myself on YouTube, which was, as TikTok is now, 'where it was at'. I protested vehemently that I didn't think it would work for me; that I would just talk for hours about what I had learnt about feminism that week and people would get bored. 'Great, do that!' they said. I felt uneasy, but decided I would just give it a go. I filmed a few videos and they did ok. I am sure if I had carried on I could've mastered it and I am sure I would have become good enough to make enjoyable vlogs, but I felt massively resistant to investing my time and energy into a YouTube channel, one of the biggest reasons being that I feared just how intrusive it seemed. Being friends with YouTubers and cameoing in their videos meant I was privy to what was going on behind the scenes.

I noticed that often when we hung out it was hard to tell if it was for hanging out's sake or for content. Everything seemed to blur into one: when did our reality end and the content begin? It was hard to tell. This was the same with Instagram, of course, but to a lesser extent. Instagram 'mummy bloggers' and couple and family accounts weren't what they are now, but that sort of content *was* big on YouTube. It concerned me. I tried to imagine filming videos of my daily life; filming me with a boyfriend; sharing those intimate moments with my audience. When people do it well, you feel like you're meant to be watching, like it's the most natural thing in the world, but all I could think about was when the filming stopped. What then? Do you immediately rewatch the footage then go your separate ways? Or do you put the camera down and enter your non-digital universe together? If not, would it be worth it to broadcast your relationship, sacrificing that quality time for views?

This was undoubtedly a 'me' issue. It's one that I can't put my finger on, because whilst I don't mind oversharing about myself and can be pretty shameless about airing my dirty laundry, I feel like I have an old-fashioned, almost sacred view of sharing too much of my relationships, romantic or otherwise, for work. What's more, I didn't enjoy the process of actually creating the video, the editing, cutting and production side. I liked telling stories and writing anecdotally in my captions, but I felt strongly that I wanted to move away from the ultra-personal content and find something outside myself to share. On a much more trivial, vanity metric, I also hated watching myself on camera. I never felt comfortable with how I looked. I couldn't seem to hold the camera at the right angle and, as far as I had come in my body acceptance journey, watching and editing endless footage of myself just didn't appeal to me.

Another issue I was having was that one of the most lucrative spaces in the influencer world is fashion, specifically fast fashion, but by the time I was in a place to monetise my style, I had already decided to boycott fast fashion and try to shop more sustainably. That meant I was inadvertently cutting off a huge revenue stream from brand deals and affiliate links, even though a few of my friends at the time were making tens of thousands of pounds a month from them. Ironically, though Instagram is what had made me habitually buy fast fashion in the first place, it was thanks to influencers-turned-activists such as Venetia La Manna that I eventually gave it up.

I have now, not without first world 'struggle' or sacrifice, come full circle with my shopping habits. When I was a little girl, I always looked to my mum for style inspiration. She's quirky and effortlessly chic; she's not afraid of a wacky shoe or a funky coat; and she always chooses personal stylistic flair over current trends. She taught me the joy of vintage shopping, the importance of good tailoring and the crime that is a flimsy lining. She knows when something is well made, when a fabric will last and what works for her. She never had the sort of disposable income I do now and she shopped sustainably out of necessity. As a result, when it comes to finding a bargain she is undoubtedly the most skilful person I have ever met, and when it comes to maintaining a wardrobe, my mum, Olive, is the blueprint. If a white item becomes yellowy and tired, she'll dye it a darker colour and give it a new lease of life. If only I hadn't let myself be tempted by eight-pound ruched-side pencil skirts and tie-me-any-way dresses, I would have a wardrobe full of evergreen second-hand designer and one-offs. Instead, I have a guilty conscience for all the spandex I sent to landfill in my early twenties. I live less than a fifteen-minute walk from her childhood home, on my own in a flat that's only a tiny bit smaller than the one she grew up in with her three brothers, mother and father.

Fashion has always been an important part of my identity, but the seeds for throwaway fashion, in particular, were planted when I was at school, when a trip to Primark became a weekend leisure activity for me and my friends. Although Primark opened its first store in the UK in 1973, I wasn't aware of it being hugely popular until I was a teenager. Where once my friends and I would spend hours in Big Topshop (RIP) on Oxford Street, taking photos of clothes we would try on in the changing rooms but never buy, leaving only with a pot of cherry Blistex as a souvenir, Primark was somewhere we could splash our teen cash. Back then we couldn't get enough faux cashmere v-neck jumpers that came in baby pinks and blues; long, tight tee-shirts that we'd fashion into mini dresses with the help of stretchy belts; and boys' grey trackies that we would inexplicably accessorise with the same stretchy belts and Ugg boots. I never thought I'd see the day this style made a comeback and thankfully I haven't seen any stretchy belts on the catwalks . . . yet. Primark wasn't the most fashionable, but it was cheap and everyone could afford it.

However, it wasn't until I moved to London that I really felt an immense pressure, greater than that of my peers outside of the industry, to document my outfits online and avoid the dreaded 'outfit repeat'. As to begin with my content was mostly fitness-related, I regularly wore the same leggings and bra combo, but for the most part wearing the same few gym outfits on rotation wasn't as much of a cardinal sin as it was with your day-to-day fashion. This changed when I moved to Brixton and got invited to those glitzy events. I started to feel the pressure to constantly present 'newness'. Our relationship with fashion in the twenty-first century is cyclical and self-fulfilling. We want new clothes all the time, but high volume and turnover mean we need lower cost, and lower cost means lower quality, so we don't invest much in our wardrobe, care less for the items and, ultimately, they have a very short life span.

Sustainable or mindful shopping is at odds with the fast-paced, digitally documented world that we live in, whereas fast fashion and social media are symbiotic. A lot of the time audiences buy things on the recommendation of an influencer to feel closer to them and their lifestyle – 'Maybe if I buy this grey hoody I will feel more like Molly-Mae?' – and this is easier when the products are cheap and accessible. It creates an attainable and tangible connection between the creator and their follower. For an influencer to truly make it, they need an invested audience and a strong brand image that people will want to buy into, so that brands want to buy real estate on your page in the form of adverts. One of the best ways to get a brand's attention is to organically feature them in your content, to prove that you love their product and are a genuine customer. Perhaps a young girl buys some items from PrettyLittleThing and she does a YouTube haul video that generates a lot of views. PLT then offers her an affiliate link, so it's in her interest to keep ordering items as she not only makes money on the views, but also every time someone makes a purchase through her link. Eventually, PLT gift her the items so she has no expenditure on the items, only the time spent creating the content and finally, if she becomes successful enough, PLT may even pay her to promote their clothes.

Now the truth is that very few people, in the grand scheme of things, manage to make a healthy living from social media. However, it is obviously a lot more alluring, rewarding and enjoyable to film fast-fashion hauls from the comfort of your own home than it is to hang up clothes in the back of a River Island or pour pints for lecherous men in a sticky-floored pub – speaking from experience. With an increasingly competitive job market, the desire for agency and the elusive goal of becoming a girlboss, it looks like a get-rich-quick fix, as Symeon Brown discusses so eloquently in his book *Get Rich or Lie Trying*. It's no wonder that so many women (and men) see influencing fast fashion brands as a route to success.

It wasn't just the cheap prices, high turnover of styles and quick delivery times that drew my generation to clothes from PrettyLittleThing, Boohoo and Missguided, but also the fact that we were now all creating a digital archive of our lives. It was in my third year of university that every single girl I knew started posting a 'pre-night-out photo'. Usually with a gin in hand, we would pose against a grimy white wall in our dilapidated university digs in another new stretchy dress. The look would not be complete without a pair of New Look beige 'suede' sandals, usually stained from a previous excursion. Almost immediately, this photo-taking became ceremonious. It was part of the night out itself. For as long as going out has existed, I imagine someone has proclaimed that getting ready is the fun part. It's a belief I share, so it doesn't surprise me how effortlessly the pre-night out photo became part of our routine. It is exactly why fast fashion brands focussed on those going out outfits and exactly why they began to boom. If you're going out three times a week (or five to six times, as I was) and you're posting your outfit each time, and you've already gone through all of your housemates' wardrobes, then of course it makes sense to order a load of dresses which cost less than a double vodka soda lime to wear once and never again. As journalist Lucy Siegle says in the documentary *The True Cost*, 'Fast fashion isn't free. Someone somewhere is paying for it.'

Ask anyone a few years ago, and the sentiment would often be that if you didn't get a picture in it yesterday, you can wear it again today. Newness is often more important than style, with impact counting for more than sartorial elegance. The rise of the Croc is a great example of how influencers can turn something from hideous to hot in a matter of months. To be fair, they are really comfy, so I for one am grateful to the pioneers of Croc rehabilitation, but whilst influencers often dress for the Gram, with outfits becoming more and more extreme to capture our easily distracted gaze, it can be shocking to see some of these screen-friendly garments out in the wild. I personally have bought outfits specific- ally for how they will look through the lens, whilst knowing I'd never wear them out to dinner. I bought one of the skin-tight cut-out Poster Girl dresses to wear for a comedy gig and remember feeling like it wasn't actually appropriate to wear such a thing out of the house. However, we all soon became immune to that as every girl on *Love Island* was dressed in one around the firepit and I ended up wearing it to a friend's birthday brunch last year. But like Andy's cerulean blue jumper in *The Devil Wears Prada*, the influencers at the top, who dress to shock, impress and engage, perhaps never envisage that versions of their barely-there get-up will make it into the mainstream lexicon of fashion. They are costumes, adornments, part of the theatre of social media. The platform is the stage and we, the influencers, are the actors, vying for the audience's attention.

How we experience things has been irrevocably changed with the advent of great camera phones; not just the clothes we choose, from 'dopamine dressing' to nostalgic Y2K outfits and barely-there dresses, but also the way we experience, well, everything. It's as though we only appreciate a moment when we capture it, its value contained solely in the ability to share it with the world. When you see people at concerts nowadays, everyone is watching and singing along, but there is a new element. Arm outstretched, phone attached, they are recording what their eyes should be watching, but instead are watching through a lens. I am entirely guilty of this and maybe it's worse because of my job. Perceiving things like this does feel very new, but when I think about it, in my lifetime I have always taken photos, if not to the same extent, then at least with the same fervour. First it was disposable cameras that we'd purchase from Boots and forget about for months or sometimes years, only to get them developed and find half the photos completely indistinct. Then came the digital camera, which we would diligently strap to our wrist on nights out in our chiffon mini dresses and strappy shoes, uploading hundred-strong albums of pictures to Facebook, never editing them or even auditing which ones were appropriate. Then, finally, the camera phone, now so advanced it seems pointless to bother buying a *real* camera.

Our school ball was such an event that every year we would sit in the school library eagerly awaiting the photos of the dresses that the sixth form girls that year had worn. It was, in many ways, our Met Gala. There was fake tanning, jewellery, new shoes – often the culmination of months of preparation. Some girls had their dresses made, others wore high-end designer and others bought them in boutiques abroad, hoping this would mean they didn't turn up in the same Topshop dress as someone else. I awaited my school ball pics with anticipation, but where photos of us were once finite in opportunity yet abundant in variety, we now have the ability to take hundreds if not thousands of photos every single day. I have to date, one hundred and twenty-six thousand, six hundred and thirty-four photos on my phone. Of that I have nine thousand, seven hundred and twenty-seven favourites. These pictures of me are the ones that may eventually end up on my grid. For every photo I post there are anything from five to five hundred near identical ones that never make the cut. If you'd have told me when I was at school that I could make thousands of pounds simply from posting photos of myself online, I would've jumped at the opportunity. The reality is often much more complicated and, frequently, much less enjoyable than it may seem.

On 30 April 2018 I sent a WhatsApp to my agent:

Hi, I know you're on holiday at the minute but super stressed with this month's payments and it's genuinely getting a bit of a joke. I haven't got enough money for my rent. 3 months in a row earning less than 1k. It's not feasible having had such low income from so few brand deals for an extended period of time to get myself on my feet.

I cringe looking back at that message. How could I have been so rude? Then again, I was getting paid sometimes up to six months after having completed a job and very few brand deals that aligned with my values were coming in, despite my agency frequently asking me who I wanted to work with. Towards the end of our working relationship, my agent would often not reply to me for days or sometimes weeks on end. I was stressed to the point of tears most days, but I also knew that I had something with my platform. I knew it could be profitable, a 'real job', I just wasn't harnessing it properly.

In April 2018 I had changed my name from @the-tinytank to @uhnonee, having repeatedly touted the 'fitness is a part of my life, but not my whole life' phrase that many on the fitness-to-lifestyle influencer pipeline rehashed to oblivion. That summer, I finally terminated my contract with my first agency and represented myself for a time. Using the knowledge I had gleaned about when and how best to approach brands and the contacts I had made at events, I managed to procure paid adverts. I didn't do badly. I got myself more work than my agents had done, plus I was earning twenty percent more without their commission. The problem was Instagram, and especially its algorithm, doesn't like chameleons. To have the girl you followed for booty workouts pivot to book posts and cultural commentary can be jarring, especially if you've missed the transition, which, due to the way the algorithm chucks content at us in a seemingly random manner, is often the way. It makes it confusing for the consumer. I would love an explore feed that encouraged me to do just that – explore! Show me something I have never seen before. Engage me in a new idea, conversation, thought. However, what works for these platforms is what works for capitalism, so that's agenda-driven algorithms that push content to us that is cohesive and fundamentally encourages us to shop.

My follower growth began to slow as my content became more varied. It was much more reflective of me as a person, being slightly chaotic, sporadic and disorganised, but it made me wonder if I could make it in this Wild West industry when I was no longer focussing on weight loss and booty pics.

My account was not growing at the same speed (which was worrying to say the least, as my follower count was the only metric I had had thus far to support this job of mine) and, besides, it was still earning me far too precarious an income. Even if the odd job paid an eye-watering few thousand pounds, I couldn't keep making it stretch to cover the months of late payments and jobs that fell through in the interim. No matter how many streams of revenue I conjured up, from merch sweaters emblazoned with 'Eggstra', a nod to the 'eggporn' videos and photos that I captioned with silly puns, to taking on extra online PT clients, it was never enough. I wasn't making the same amount of money as my friends on grad schemes, even if I was eating at lavish restaurants and rubbing shoulders with Love Islanders.

That September, on a flight back from Greece, I sat with my head in my hands, crying quietly. I can't do this anymore, I thought to myself. Despite my previous gumption, it seemed that in the end everyone else would be vindicated. It was too difficult – not the actual work, but making the work I was doing viable. *I* wasn't able to make it work. I felt like I was making all the right decisions and being true to myself. I wasn't selling out and I was making difficult choices, turning down more than I was accepting, but the right thing, it seemed, was the wrong thing if you wanted to be financially successful.

As the old adage goes, all that glitters is not gold. Earlier that year I had been on a press trip to Lime Wood with Very for their new Nike collection, flown to Spain with Fitbit and even hosted my very own fitness retreat in Sardinia. You're encouraged to go on these press trips, as even though they aren't paid, they're great for building brand relationships and, of course, they're fun. You can create content when you're there, too, so technically you're not missing out on work, and there's the plus that they provide all your food and board, so once again I was skint, but living lavishly. When I went to Japan with Asics, I met PT, yoga instructor and fitness influencer extraordinaire Shona Vertue on the plane. We spent the entire eighteen-hour flight talking about our industry, about how it needed to change and our goals for the future. She told me that she was managed by a feminist talent agency, who didn't so much prioritise the commercial digital side, but instead cultivated you as an individual and helped you create work that was true to you. I slightly fell in love with Shona, as everyone who meets her does, and asked for her agency's details. After the forty-eight hour round trip to Kyoto, where Shona, a few other influencers and I were lucky enough to run along Sakura-lined rivers, eat traditional sushi and practise meditation, I emailed her agent, Francesca, but heard nothing back.

I had decided that if by the end of the year things were still too stressful, I would go back to the drawing board. I was still only twenty-four, I had plenty of time to start again. I don't think I had told friends or family how much I was struggling, plus I was gifting people experiences or products that I myself had been gifted, which made me look like I could afford to be extravagant and generous. From the outside looking in, my life looked so easy and so much fun.

We all know there's no such thing as a free lunch, but when it comes to influencers it may seem as though the streets are paved with gifts, money grows on swipe up links (I guess it sort of does), and brunches are whipped up whenever we enter a café. The gifting process is an enigma to many, but if it seems like it's too good to be true, that's because it is. When a brand sends an influencer something, they're doing it in the hopes they will post it. It's not so much a 'gift' as a transaction. The brand only incurs the cost of the product plus postage, rather than having to pay for the advertising space for their product, which would cost substantially more. This means sometimes a thousand times return, sometimes more, on advertising spend, but whilst that's fantastic for brands and an undeniable perk of having an audience, sadly you can't pay your bills in gifts.

Today, I get very little volume-wise in the way of gifts. A few years ago, around the same time that I started on my sustainable fashion journey, I asked PRs to stop sending me gifts without having asked me first. Things just used to turn up, piles of products, usually with lots of packaging and paper for press releases. I would find myself walking to the post office with piles of red slips not knowing what I was going to pick up or who had sent it. PRs would add you to gifting lists and then from there it was potluck who would end up with your home address. I gave most of it to friends, family and charity shops, but after a while the sheer amount of unwanted stuff ending up on my doorstep was staggering. I had a box under my bed filled with beauty products for anyone who came round to rifle through and take what they liked or I'd donate it to women's charities. Where on earth were they expecting me to put it all? Like the parties, it was exciting at first, but as time went on it made me view material possessions differently; it made me realise just how pointless a lot of it truly was. I still receive gifts, sometimes things that I simply cannot believe I have been given, but other than that it's mostly books dropping through my letter box or items from small sustainable fashion brands that I am all too happy to post about unpaid.

But in 2018, when I was still being gifted endless water bottles and protein bars, I hoped those gifts were a sign that I was doing *something* right. I was working hard, spending every waking hour creating, engaging and reacting, all the while online coaching and tirelessly reaching out to podcast guests, but as ever not really knowing what I was doing or to what end. I was, at least, enjoying myself. Even if what I was doing wasn't working from a commercial point of view, I was in my element. I spoke to my audience day in day out, responding to DMs, speaking on my stories, engaging in debate. Everything was immediate, instant. I was in that sense, the perfect influencer. Always plugged in.

The week after my mini meltdown on the plane back from Greece, I reached out to a few PT studios in South-West London and found a part-time position at a fancy gym in Clapham Junction. With this new role, I had a bit more structure to my days and a concrete source of income. Whilst I loved working with clients, I didn't enjoy being around some of the male personal trainers. The IRL fitness industry, it seemed, had not caught up with the online one. I resolved to make it work anyway. I needed a stable supplementary income to support a new venture that was very close to my heart.

Chapter 5

A FEW MONTHS prior, just as I had reached an impasse with my agents, they said, 'What about a podcast?' My ears pricked up. Of course, that was what my next content stream should be. They were the ones to suggest the title *Adulting*, as my content ever since I had moved to London had been very graduate-centric, trying to find myself in an adult world. They were imagining conversations on inane tasks like how to keep your whites white, the best ways to make your rented flat feel like a home, how to pay your bills and other fairly straightforward adulting tasks. All of these are easily shoppable and sponsorable, and I could see the pound signs in my agents' eyes. My generation coined the term adulting to much derision. Everyone else had figured out how to just get on with things. Why did millennials have to be so inept and lazy? It was a pandemic of its own, all of us satirising our lack of home-making skills, but also a broader comment on the load that we were undertaking.

Once the idea for *Adulting* became more fleshed out and I felt confident that I understood where I wanted to go with it, I started to feel more dubious about my relationship with the agency. On commission, they wanted a fifty-fifty split on the podcast in return for producing and packaging the series, but I was starting to worry about being too tied in to them when I wasn't entirely sure that we were that well aligned.

On 9 February 2018 I sent a WhatsApp to my agent:

Just thinking about the podcast and I definitely think I'd like to have a go at editing and doing it on my own, just because listening to that first one there's stuff included/not included that I would have done differently and I just really want full autonomy over content and I feel like I can't have that without editing it. So let me know when I could come in next week and I can have a go recording on my own!

I really want you to trust me on this one. I listen to so many podcasts and I really understand what my audience will be expecting of me. This podcast will be my biggest project and I want us to feel like we're working together. Right now, I feel a little bit like I'm being backed into a corner, so I'd really love to be given the reins and make this the successful podcast we want it to be x

On 14 March 2018 I published a three-minute trailer via a podcast platform called Anchor. On 9 April 2018 it was No. 1 on Apple iTunes podcast charts and continued to hover near the top every time I released an episode. At this point it wasn't generating any revenue and despite personal training, online coaching and plugging away tirelessly at my social media content I was still struggling to make ends meet. Basically, I started *Adulting* sort of running before I could walk. The idea was that I wanted to explore the world through other people's eyes. I was curious and I had become comfortable in positioning myself as someone with more questions than answers. The podcast soon adopted the tagline 'All of the things we never got taught in school' and the first episode was with my mum. I titled it 'The Podmother: Millennial meets Baby Boomer' (it is the one of most listened to episodes).

In the beginning, I started off by recording on a microphone that I had reluctantly bought off Amazon for three hundred pounds. I really couldn't afford it at the time, but because I hadn't signed the fifty-fifty deal with my then agents, they wouldn't let me use theirs. I invited guests to my Brixton Hill flat and we recorded out of my living room. The sound quality was dreadful and garnered quite a few not unwarranted complaints in the reviews section on Apple Podcasts. To cut costs, I tried to teach myself how to use audio-editing software called Audacity, but before long I gave in and hired a producer to do the absolute minimum and edit the audio quality for me. I continued to edit the actual content and do the rest of the production myself. Initially, I was sort of terrible at it. I interrupted guests and pre-empted their answers, always eager to participate and share my point of view, which also resulted in negative reviews on the podcast. Eventually, after the initial ego-hit, I took the comments on board as constructive criticism.

However, by late 2018 *Adulting* had really started to take off. I was booking guests I could've only dreamt of and getting sponsorships from brands and institutions that not only aligned with the podcast, but also felt like they had a bigger meaning beyond monetary value. On 28 November I checked the stats and my podcast had gained over one-million downloads. I posted this to my story and the podcast hosting giant Acast got in touch. The following January I signed a contract with them to host *Adulting*, which meant they would find sponsorship for the podcast so it could start generating revenue. Soon after this I signed with my second talent agency. It wasn't Shona's agent, but the woman who was to manage me was intelligent, interesting and had a very similar outlook to me. We got along really well, but the problem was she worked for a huge commercial agency and, even if we were on the same page personally, the umbrella company was very similar to my last. Nevertheless, we worked together to find a way to move me away from the fitness niche. Thankfully, due to the podcast I was no longer seen by brands as just a fitness influencer.

As time went on I got better at listening rather than interrupting, as well as asking the right questions, and I was able to access quite high-profile guests. I started to rent a studio space in the centre of Soho on an ad hoc basis or sometimes I'd go into the Acast offices and record in their in-house podcast studio. Just like with Instagram, I seemed to be in the right place with the right idea at just the right time. *Adulting* had a solid listenership and tapped into an ever-growing conversation about identity and privilege in ways that felt open and productive. Not only was I getting sponsorships from brands like Sweaty Betty, who previously wouldn't touch my Instagram with a bargepole, but I also worked with the NHS, the Department for Education and Public Health England. I was unequivocally proud of what I had created and the fact that I was getting my teeth stuck into partnerships that would have a broader, more ethical impact than the protein powder partnerships that could have awaited me.

When it came to guests, one of the most notable for me at the time was Sara Pascoe. She had been on my list right at the beginning before the podcast even existed. I had reached out a few times, but it was only after the podcast became more established that I finally heard back. This was extremely affirming for me. I started to become more comfortable about the future of my career. If I chipped away slowly at the things I was interested in, I thought, and kept everything else ticking over, eventually that hard work would pay off. I spent hours collating emails for agents, reaching out to friends who might have connections to certain industries, and tirelessly shooting my shot with people who had no idea who I was. I soon learnt that there was safety in numbers. If I emailed fifty people, maybe ten would get back to me and maybe three would agree to appear. Even then, with the higher-profile guests especially, there was the risk they'd just cancel or rearrange last minute, sometimes hours before recording, when I had already booked and paid for a studio. It was a gamble and I was investing every penny I earned from Instagram and coaching into funding it, but in the end it paid off.

Once *Adulting* started to generate revenue, I finally had some financial stability and independence. It was giving me a monthly 'salary', something I had never had before, plus I was still getting an income from personal training and occasional adverts on my Instagram. 'Multiple avenues for revenue,' a friend had once told me, 'is the key to being successfully self-employed.' It seemed I had achieved a trifecta. What a relief it was to finally be free from weeks of guessing when I would receive my next paycheque. I hadn't really anticipated *Adulting* becoming a reliable income stream. In fact, in hindsight, the reason I believe *Adulting* worked was because for the first time in a long while I felt like I was doing something valuable again. I hadn't started a podcast to make money; it was born out of an organic desire to create something that would be positive, useful and needed. I was interviewing guests about all the different cultural, socio-economic and socio-political aspects that impact our lives, as well as learning about lots of the things that many of us professed we never got taught in school. The topics ranged from friendships in your twenties to money management to feminism and structural racism. I felt so lucky not only be able to interview people who inspired me personally, but also to share these conversations with the world.

My audience was immediately receptive. Most of them were women my age, living in the UK. We had had similar experiences, and we were entering our graduate lives in a country that seemed more divided and divisive than ever. We were grappling with taking on financial responsibilities and learning to maintain a home, and at the same time living through what felt like quite a tumultuous time. Keeping up with changing cultural landscapes and constant political unrest felt like a full-time job, so podcasts like *The High Low* were immensely popular. They condensed the biggest stories of the week into digestible information and added levity through pop-culture analysis, too. As much as it was teaching me about others, it also taught me a lot about myself, my privileges and my place in this structurally unfair society.

This more intellectual avenue of work was starting to create a disjunct between the persona I portrayed in the static images of my Instagram feed and the conversations I was hosting on my podcast. Once again, I couldn't work out how to translate the real me on to an image-sharing platform. Around this time, video content was becoming more commonplace and the long captions I had cut my teeth on were starting to die out. I stuck with the long captions, as did many of my original cohort of influencers, but soon Instagram was too fast paced and evolving beyond this sort of content. For me, this was ok. I had my podcast for those longer form conversations, plus the occasional live podcast and my monthly book club, where I could engage with my followers IRL and really get to know them. I felt like I was building something bigger. For a while now, Instagram had acted more as a hub for keeping up with my audience and sharing things that aligned to the lifestyle influencer box I had migrated into, but I was still searching for more.

With any sort of creative job there is this feeling that because it is so enjoyable it isn't truly work. Sitting behind a microphone and chatting to someone you really admire for an hour is not the same as doing hard labour or teaching children or looking after sick patients. I went from hounding ad agencies begging for payments to cover my rent to suddenly earning almost double what my friends were earning, and Emily, five years my senior and a doctor, was getting paid a fraction of my income. It's difficult to acknowledge and uncomfortable to talk about a faulty system that underpays teachers, doctors, cleaners and people in all those jobs the pandemic has taught us are essential when I profit from it.

As it stands, I will do anything to disguise the fact that I am an influencer. If a stranger asks me about my job, I might say, 'Oh, I am a content creator' or 'I work in social media' before making my excuses and finding someone who knows me and who I don't need to explain myself to. When I first downloaded dating apps after coming out of that four-year relationship with Z, it made me cringe to see that many replies to the prompt, 'Don't date me . . .' were 'if you're an influencer' or 'you want to be an influencer' or even 'you like social media'. I hate being tarred with a brush that I don't think applies to me. I'm not like other ~~girls~~ influencers *eye roll emoji*. (I'm kidding – I am just like every other girl, but that's something to be proud of, because girls are great.) The more the term influencer becomes mainstream, the more the public image of us is solidified into a monolith, which seems to consist of young ex *Love Islanders*, *Geordie Shore* alumni and Kardashian-Jenners. Of course, they are all influencers and I follow many of them, too, but like the cliques in a noughties chick-flick, we all have different styles and outlooks, and populate different corners of our dining hall known as the internet. I'm inclined to agree with author and journalist Caroline O'Donoghue, who, on a recent episode of her podcast *Sentimental Garbage*, commented that 'saying you hate influencers is like saying you hate pop music'. It's an anodyne statement that says more about someone's complete lack of knowledge of the breadth of the industry than it does about us.

One day I decided I wanted to get an insight into what people genuinely thought about influencers. Perhaps it was just the media bad-mouthing my profession rather than a commonly held sentiment. I did a poll on my Insta stories and asked my audience what their first thought was when they heard the word. Whilst the responses were varied, the majority mentioned fast fashion, fakery and free stuff. Almost all were negative, but often with the caveat that, despite this, they didn't view *me* like that; that I was different. With my ego sufficiently stroked, fluffed and reassured, I re-read the responses. It was so interesting to see how many of them had one definition for the word, but then pointed out the people that they follow, who technically fitted the description of influencer as someone who was making money from their platform, didn't fall into the description they'd provided. In Rutger Bregman's *Utopia for Realists*, he talks about the concept of bullshit jobs and, no, he isn't talking about influencers, he's talking about bankers: 'In a world that's getting even richer, where cows produce more milk and robots produce more stuff, there's more room for friends, family, community service, science, art, sports, and also room for more bullshit. As long as we continue to be obsessed with work, work, and more work (even as useful activities are further automated or outsourced), the number of superfluous jobs will only continue to grow'.[4] So, fair enough, I am not saying *my* page (especially not on its own and especially not while I have been writing this book) necessarily offers ground-breaking content, and the metrics in which I make my money are directly tied into consumption, production and capitalism . . . but if we look at the content being produced across all platforms there are some genius artists in their own right. The skill of YouTubers such as Emma Chamberlain, the wit of TikTok comedians like, for instance, Munya Chawawa, the poets, podcasters, designers and creatives who use social media to share their work (often free to consume) – when you look at it like that, I think social media might just incubate some of the least bullshit jobs around.

One of the responses from my audience that really made me laugh, however, was that influencer to them just meant, 'Sales for theatre kids'. It amused me because I think it's pretty on the nose. Many of the women that were in my cohort of fitness influencers six or seven years ago, like Alice Liveing or Tally Rye, did have a background in theatre or performing, as did I,

---

[4] *Utopia for Realists*, Rutger Bregman, Bloomsbury, 2017.

although not to any particularly impressive standard. Influencing is a performance, in a way; a performance of the self, but a performance nonetheless. And I *love* performing.

Something else I found refreshing about focussing on the podcast was that my income was not so directly tied to my appearance. By this point, influencers were a proper thing, so much so that it wasn't just girls in their university dorm rooms posting mirror selfies with piles of laundry just out of shot, but high production value content brought to you by women who looked like they had walked out of the pages of the very magazines that were now becoming obsolete because of them. People were making real money and, as a result, more money was being poured into the content that they were creating. It was the era of Adobe Light Room pre-sets that made everyone's feed have that expensive *Made in Chelsea* glow.

Suddenly, an industry built on 'authenticity' and 'relatability' was becoming polished and commercialised. Not only this, but non-invasive cosmetic procedures (or 'tweakments' as people now refer to them), as well as full cosmetic surgery and photo-editing, were on the rise. Where once Botox and fillers were for celebrities and movie stars, more and more 'normal' people were going under the knife – and the needle. Especially, it seemed, in the influencer communities. Instagram filters on stories had really taken off, most notably the ones that subtly smoothed your skin or slimmed your nose or plumped your lips or usually all three. In an episode of *Adulting* where I spoke with dermatologist Anjali Mahto, she told me how she now had clients coming in asking to have procedures to make them look how they did with the filters on. And a new phenomenon was born: 'Instagram face'. As Jia Tolentino wrote in 2019, 'The human body is an unusual sort of Instagram subject: it can be adjusted, with the right kind of effort, to perform better and better over time.' In the essay she goes on to elaborate on 'the gradual emergence, among professionally beautiful women, of a single, cyborgian face'.[5]

I'm sure you can imagine exactly what she's talking about. It is inescapable, this look. From models like Kendall Jenner and Bella Hadid to influencer sisters like Isabelle and Olivia Mathers, and countless others. Just as the Kardashian silhouette redefined the ideal body shape, so, too, did this very specific combination of features become the holy grail of 'face cards'. Where in some cases it may be a fortuitous design of nature, in others it seemed more than likely to be the opposite of divine intervention. Just as I had climbed out of one insecurity-ridden existence, another was beginning to creep up on me. It wasn't enough to be girl-next-door pretty, wearing mismatched thrifted outfits and poorly applied eyeliner. If I wanted to make it as an influencer,

---

[5] 'The Age of Instagram Face', Jia Tolentino, *New Yorker*, December 2019.

apparently, the requirements had changed. I needed pore-less skin, designer handbags, and a designer face.

I spoke candidly to my audience about this conflict brewing within me; about wanting to show up to discuss varied issues and share snippets about my life, but that having to be front-facing all the time and appear 'attractive' was becoming a heavier burden. This has been the affliction of women in the media since, well, forever. If we want to deliver information to an audience, we have to do so in a pretty package – men, not so much. The more visible you are, the more likely you are to feel the pressure of new trends and paradigms, but you're also more likely to have the access to achieve them. There's a sort of trickledown effect, which may not work in economics, but in the beauty economy, it sure does. There's a hierarchy of who gets impacted by these beauty standards first, but eventually they seep into everything and everyone. Those without a large Instagram audience aren't unaffected. On the contrary, it seems the closer influencers come to celebrity status, the more the pressure gap between influencer and non-influencer seems to shrink. Because their appearances and lifestyles start off as somewhat attainable, once influencers begin to get procedures or buy expensive products, their audiences also feel that their aesthetic should be progressing at the same, often unrealistic, rate. Ironically, as I started to earn more money in the following years, and started to be gifted more expensive items of clothing and beauty products, I found it easier to maintain a level of appearance that made me feel more comfortable in front of the camera. As the meme goes, 'You're not ugly, just broke.' I tend not to worry as much about my appearance these days, probably mostly because of learning how to do my makeup properly and, gratefully, just through getting older. I do sometimes have mild panics about the wrinkles threatening to cement themselves into my face and the way my boobs are definitely two inches lower than they were a few years ago, but for the most part, aging has proved to be more a process of feeling more secure about myself, not less.

I had been having conversations with my audience about how my feminism conflicted with my desire to subscribe to certain beauty ideals, and how social media played into this, when *Women's Health* reached out to me to ask if I would be interested in writing an article for them about 'the psyche of social media'. Reader, I was psyched . . . pardon the pun. I forwarded it to my agent, asking what she thought about it, and she picked up the conversation, asking what the feature would be and if I would be paid. It was to be a six-page spread in the middle of the printed issue, two thousand words with professionally shot photos of me as an accompaniment. I had been trying to get more freelance writing gigs, having written a few pieces for the now defunct online mag *Drugstore*, so although it turned out to be one of the many false starts I have experienced in my career, this invitation to write for such a big publication felt like another win I had manifested.

I couldn't believe it. Someone wanted me to write for them about my experiences and expertise, and it wasn't because of how I looked, but because they thought I was knowledgeable and capable. This was heartening on two directly opposing levels. On the one hand, I was bored of being perceived as a vapid influencer, on the other, I was worried that I was no longer attractive enough to *be* an influencer. It felt like an olive branch from the industry, a rare opportunity to shed some light on the positives that I encountered every day as a young online content creator.

I was still very enamoured with social media at this point, even if I couldn't quite work out how I fitted into it. And I was still seeking the apex of my feminist learning journey, believing that I was acting as an agent for change, an ambassador for the future generation who were surely going to change the world for the better. The title pitched to me was 'Unpicking the psyche of social media', but the intention of the article wasn't quite what it first seemed. It turned out the article wasn't to be about what I thought of the psyche of social media, after all. It was about me, but not my opinions, rather my psyche, and whether I, as a representative of influencers, was a narcissist. They asked me to interview a leading psychologist on what narcissistic personality disorder (NPD) really was and I gathered information on why we shouldn't be throwing that term around so flippantly, as well as sharing anecdotal stories that they sort of nudged me towards, that framed 'the Instagrammable' as something from *Black Mirror*. Don't get me wrong, sometimes it does feel like that, but there were hundreds of think pieces on this aspect and I wanted to share something fresh, something hopeful.

And then there were the photographs. For the shoot, they styled me in Calvin Klein underwear and trainers, and asked me to take photos in a mirror or pretend to be taking selfies. I was a bit confused that the shoot was in underwear, as it didn't seem to have anything to do with the piece, but it was *Women's Health*, I reasoned with myself. I asked in no uncertain terms not to be Photoshopped or airbrushed and this, at least, was honoured. They read me the piece over the phone, but said they would be unable to send me a written copy of the final edit. I can't remember the reason for this now. I tried to jot down bits as the journalist narrated it back to me, but overall it was quite difficult to recall what she said without seeing it in writing. When they finally sent it to me, they said no edits could be made as it had already been sent to the printers. The title was 'Am I *really* a narcissist?' and the introduction read:

> The term – used technically to describe someone with a legitimate personality disorder – has become shorthand for describing anyone with a taste for selfies and self-reflection. But is it fair? Influencer Oenone Forbat – whose business model is built on her appearance and personality – goes in search of answers.

I immediately WhatsApped the article to a journalist friend of mine:

> Fuck just got my Women's Health piece and I think they've made me sound awful . . . They cut out loads of bits where I talk about how social media helps with activism, and how it's not about what u look like etc/I wrote a totally different piece,/ The stuff I properly wanted to talk about is gone.

She answered, 'I guarantee you that way more people look at your Insta than read *Women's Health*,' and she was right. They say all publicity is good publicity, but I never shared the piece. Despite having spoken about it in the lead-up on my stories, and even posting behind-the-scenes pictures from the shoot on my feed, save for a few people who DM'd me to say they'd read the article and loved it, the piece went for the most part under the radar. Reading it back now, it's quite good, actually. It touches on a lot of things I talk about in this book, but I still have a seedling of resentment for feeling I was set up. Even though the article is interesting, the framing and photoshoot still feels derisive, if not a little degrading.

At the end of 2019, my new best friend at the time and forever best friend now, comedian, author and smutty-humoured Grace Campbell, encouraged me to give comedy a go. We met when I had her as a guest on

Adulting that summer and have barely gone a day without speaking since. She invited me to perform at her Disgraceful Club, a comedy night she was hosting at the Box nightclub in Soho, where she headlined and platformed up-and-coming comedians as well as well-established ones. Without her, I would never have found my next great love. Having been online for so long without finding my perfect niche, it was a delight to work away at a new craft in dark dingy pubs before tiny audiences, who neither knew who I was nor cared. All I had to do was make them laugh. That is by no means a small feat, but it was a much clearer objective than managing and maintaining a platform to satisfy over a hundred thousand people. Every gig I have ever done, whether it was to raptured applause or pin-drop silence, left me fizzing and full. I had always been a huge comedy fan, having spent years avidly watching *Mock The Week*, *Live At The Apollo*, *Would I Lie to You?* and every stand-up special available, but it had never occurred to me that I could just try it out myself.

This left me with more questions than answers. Having had almost as many career pivots as I had had ex-boyfriends, I felt that surely comedy couldn't also be *the one*, just like fitness was and then podcasts? Once again, the more I dipped my toe into the comedy pond, the more it made sense to me. It drew together social commentary, topical observations and performance, all of which I loved. The thrill of having a whole room laugh at a joke that you've crafted and honed is something I believe everyone should experience at least once in their lives. Prior to *Adulting* my content on Instagram had usually erred on the side of humorous and tongue in cheek; however, as the podcast started to enter into more complicated and serious subject matter, so too did my online persona. I am naturally disposed to be too earnest and sincere if I am not watching myself, or if I have had a glass of wine instead of a tequila ginger beer.

Once again, I still felt the weight of needing to micro-manage myself across all platforms, to present one consolidated and easily digestible brand. It was like I existed across two planes, personal and public, and whenever one was going well the other suffered.

Chapter 6

AT THE BEGINNING of 2020, much like everyone else, I had many, many plans for greatness. In January I signed with a new talent agency; my third and hopefully final one, the Found; the same agency that Shona had told me about two years prior. Serendipitously, Francesca had seen me perform my first ever five minutes of stand-up and had asked a colleague, 'Who is this Oenone girl?' 'It's that TinyTank that always emails us,' came the reply. Francesca saw something in me that she hadn't been able to glean from my feed and she was confident she had the tools to make others see it too. As Francesca put it to me, 'When you look at your Instagram, who are you?' and she was right, it was a mess. But with her help, we were going to change that. It was to be My! Year! I was going to improve my social media, tour my book club and podcast around the UK, start a series of live talks and, ultimately, break free from the label of influencer. I would still be one, but it would appear lower down the list of my millennial accolades.

Then Covid happened. Emily, being a doctor, put the fear of God into me about the pandemic before the scaremongering had really set in nationally. I sent myself into lockdown a week before we were legally obliged to, missing a friend's birthday and other social events that would turn out to be the last hurrah for much longer than any of us knew back then. I had been with Z for just two years at this point and I was living alone in Streatham Hill, but we decided that he should move in during lockdown, which we thought might just be for three weeks, not the best part of two years on and off. I didn't feel ready to move in with him yet, but it made sense given the situation and soon we were cooking together, doing yoga together, watching *Tiger King* together . . . It was exciting and comforting to play at being grown-ups amongst all the fear and chaos.

Everyone was online and lots of people were furloughed, so I logged in and never really logged off. Having always worked from home I realised I had an advantage, something useful to share at a time when everyone wanted to help each other. I made a shareable infographic with my top tips on how to do it successfully, which sort of went viral in a mini kind of way. I figured out how to podcast remotely and resolved to do an episode every week for as long as we were in lock-down. Perhaps this year didn't have to be a disaster after all. This went on for a month or so, until I found out I was pregnant.

I knew before I even did the test. My period was late, but I also just knew. Then again, I always 'know'. Like the time at school when I was convinced I was pregnant and made my first ever boyfriend buy me a pregnancy test from Boots in the local town at lunch-time. I waited outside, red-faced and sweaty-palmed. Back at school, I locked myself in a cubicle in the loos and peed on my first stick. It came back negative. This shouldn't have been surprising, seeing as we were both virgins. This incident somewhat summed me up; my poor boyfriend spending most of his pocket money on pregnancy tests that we really had no business buying. The truth was, I was terrified of sex. I might as well have attended Coach Carter's lecture in *Mean Girls*. I believed pregnancy was in my future if I so much as came within a metre of a penis. It was my biggest fear. My mum would never forgive me if I fell pregnant. I have worried my period is late more times than I can count, convincing myself I am pregnant and then bleed-ing the moment only one line appears. So, when I did that test on a Friday morning in late April 2020, I was stunned. I was so shocked I couldn't believe it. I had gone through these motions so many times before, but I had never been right. I was like the girl who cried wolf to herself.

'The line is so faint though?' I whispered, as it became more defined. It was unmistakably there and I knew this time, for real, I was pregnant.

I had always been pro-choice, but really because I thought I was special – and not in a good way. I thought I was too weak, too delicate, to have a baby, yet I was also concerned that an abortion would irreversibly change me. I feared my mind would romanticise the baby I'd decided not to have; that I would wake up each year on the potential due date, haunted by a child that never was. I had a friend at university who further solidified these fears by telling me she regularly imagined the child she aborted, that she wondered what they'd be like, what they'd be up to. 'They would've been nine', she told me once, as she sat on a wall opposite the university library, smoking a rollie, legs swinging. I stood opposite her holding a sandwich, looking at her intently as she gazed wistfully into the distance as though searching for the soul of the child.

I'd done so well. I'd come so far not getting pregnant – almost a decade of home runs! Getting pregnant at twenty-five whilst living with my boyfriend, well, maybe this was my time to be a mother? Of course, I wouldn't have chosen to have a baby now, but it takes two to tango, and we had tangoed and now I was pregnant. I was struggling to find reasons not to have a baby. I considered the facts and tried to be logical. I told myself I was financially stable (reader, I absolutely was not), old enough (again, in hindsight I might as well have been

12) and in a loving relationship (one that was destined to end). I don't know if it was the hormones, the quarantine, my absolute lack of pragmatism or a combination of all three, but I entered into an existential crisis of whether or not I wanted to keep a baby that I had never planned on conceiving in the first place.

Before I came to my decision, I developed a habit of taking myself away to sulk in the bedroom, completely mute. I'd lie in the dark with the blinds pulled down. I'd cradle my belly, which had rounded and softened. I knew it was from the pasta and wine nights we'd come to look forward to as our quarantine ritual, but I'd imagine the soft swell of my lower abdomen was from the burgeoning life I was incubating. It's just a bunch of cells, I would remind myself. But then I kept imagining it as a baby, my baby. I thought about going it alone. I would be a great single mother. I could live in this flat with a baby. I could do my job whilst being pregnant. It could work. Maybe I should make it work? In fact, whenever I imagined myself having the baby, it was always on my own; it was me and the baby against the world. Although he had been incredibly supportive, understanding and kind throughout, I hadn't really factored in Z at all.

I rang my agent, Francesca, who was fast becoming my confidante, voice of reason and mentor. When I told her my concerns about getting an abortion, she assured me that as you get older you will find out that 'so many people have had one'. Not just sixteen-year-olds who aren't ready, but married mothers in their forties who don't want another kid, and women in their twenties, like me, who just aren't ready yet. There is no socially unacceptable time to have an abortion, but there are only a few, very select moments when any individual truly feels ready to have a baby, and only that person can know when that is, and even then there's never really a good or right time. I immediately felt better after speaking to her, in a way that made me feel cruel to Z. Why could she console me so much better? I resolved it was because she's a woman, she's a mother, and she is older than me and wiser.

A few days later, on a sanctioned one-hour walk, I ambled down the long hill towards Brixton, turning right into Elm Park Road. This street is one of my favourites, full of pretty, colourful houses that I often used to play-imagine a future in. They looked so different today, out of focus and in sharp relief all at once. I took some photos of wisteria tumbling down the lip of a doorframe. I was wearing a lime green tank top, with a fluffy green cardigan in the same pastel hue, Levi's 501s, sunglasses and trainers. Everything was gifted except the tank and trainers, so I took some selfies to post on Instagram. I look like my mother in the photos. I kept walking until I reached the flower garden in Brockwell Park, then I sat on a bench, took a deep breath and rang Marie Stopes. Luckily, they had just announced a change in the rules that meant you were allowed to get an abortion during lockdown.

I didn't tell my mum or Emily, because what made

all of this even more confusing is that Emily was trying for a baby. I felt so much guilt and shame that I was terminating something that she would've loved to have kept. So, I cried on my own, for my fleeting belief that I too, would be a mother.

On 1 May I took the first set of tablets, which terminated the pregnancy, and on 2 May I took the second set, to expel it. The cramps were nothing short of excruciating. Z was making a chicken katsu curry from scratch to comfort me. I could smell it from the kitchen in the studio flat we shared, where, metres away, I was on all fours on the bed, groaning, deep guttural sounds that seemed to come from my womb and escape through my mouth. My instincts were to put my body in this position, to growl, to sweat. I felt like an animal, primal. I felt as though I was giving birth. I was so nauseous I couldn't eat, even though it smelt so good and I was starving, but I managed some a few hours later, with a tray propped up on a pillow on my lap in bed. I ate slower than I ever have before, exhausted, spent, drained.

A couple of days passed and I wasn't sure the clots were big enough, that I had bled enough. I was terrified it hadn't worked; that I had made the decision, but it wasn't just a simple process. I rang the clinic and they said I should go for a scan to make sure, but the only place they had an appointment was in Ealing. Public transport being off-limits, we got an Uber and arrived a little early, so we wandered around the common. Once I got inside, the clinicians were already packing up for the day. I lay on the bed as the doctor prepared the ultrasound and told me there was no pregnancy left. 'It's gone.' I was in and out in all of four minutes. A year later, I walked around the same common with Emily and her husband, and although I thought it looked so familiar, I couldn't put my finger on why. Had I been there before? I couldn't remember.

On the same day that I took the first set of Misoprostol I was due to hand in the proposal for a book that never was, whilst I bled out the bunch of cells for something that would never come to be. Before the first lockdown I was approached by a literary agent, who saw great promise in the idea of turning *Adulting* into a non-fiction book about all of the things we never got taught in school. I was flattered and excited by this proposition. We went for lunch somewhere fancy and I peacocked, as I do when I feel safe and seen. I talked about how I could theme each chapter around a school subject: chemistry could be about drugs and alcohol, biology about love and sex, geography about privilege and class, etc. Francesca had been saying I should try to write a book for some time, because the sort of career I was seeking needed more traditional media attention. Simply existing in online spaces might be incredible for commercial gain, but I had visions of writing novels, presenting, perhaps even writing sitcoms. My body of work, except for perhaps my podcast, was ephemeral. I may spend hours drafting a spoken word poem about beauty, or edit a caption ruthlessly to fit it in the word limit, but within nine days of posting consistently, it would be pushed down below the horizon of my feed, unsearchable and fundamentally in the past.

It was in the first lockdown that I started to really try and write, to work out the initial concept of what would eventually become this book. I felt as though it were an opportunity to let my audience and readers know me on a level that I had been unable to verbalise before. Social media, as we have heard everyone say, is no place for nuance, but with thousands of words to laze about in, nuance in a book is more than welcome; it is encouraged; it is the whole point. I could stretch myself out and fill myself up. This wouldn't be a one-dimensional portrayal, but a full-bodied, well-aged glass of me to be drunk and understood. Like any story, I thought it pertinent to start at the beginning. I laid my hands on the keys and I typed until my fingertips felt numb, not even realising I had started to cry. The act of trying to write 'my story' had unearthed memories and emotions that I had kept buried for the best part of the two decades I had been alive. The fact that someone had asked me, coupled with living through a pandemic that reduced our lives not only to the walls we lived in, but to the interiors of our own heads, meant I had a psychological reckoning that now I can only say I am so grateful for.

I locked the original bit of writing that I had penned on Pages, titled 'GP Book', with 'GP' standing for growing pains. That story wasn't one to be shared, it was for me to put together and help me to make sense of myself. I am so glad that it wasn't the story I ended up telling. Although this book is very personal, I have carefully considered what needs to be said and what doesn't. Having read so many authors say they regret the extremely exposing pieces of work they wrote in their twenties, I am conscious that female writers especially are often encouraged to scour the depths of their private lives and offer up their trauma to the masses. Perhaps I will look back on this in a few years and wince at my words, but I hope it won't be because I gave up more of myself than I needed to.

Despite having barely been pregnant, the hormonal ramifications of the pregnancy and subsequent termination were intense. I felt depressed for days, maybe even weeks after. I can't really remember. I just remember not being able to get out of bed. Quarantine, mixed with my first pregnancy being an unwanted one and the uncertainty of the world meant that I felt myself falling through the pillows, like I was being absorbed into the mattress, my body a weightless vessel floating above me in reality, me below in some other dimension. On 5 May I posted a poem on Instagram:

When you aren't always sure
If everything is ok
If tomorrow will be as uncertain
As it is today
Celebrate the blue skies
Commiserate with the rain

This is your life
Your landscape
Unchartered terrain
Life is such a fickle thing
One that's a pleasure to own
And if you listen to the birds sing
You'll never walk alone

I think everyone just thought I was talking about quarantine or being characteristically sentimental or trying to write new Natasha Bedingfield lyrics. If I got an abortion now (which, reader, if I fell pregnant right now, I would, a million times over), I would probably share it online. As Roe v Wade is overturned and states across the US begin to rescind the right to an abortion, it feels emotional to write about this, not because I had an abortion, but because there are people out there who will not be able to access them safely. I feel so much less ambivalent towards abortions, not only because I have had one and it was the right decision, but also because I feel so much more informed. I understand the gravity of parenthood in a way I simply didn't compute at twenty-five. Because oddly, despite my strongly held liberal views, I had somehow absorbed this idea that an abortion would scar me.

Yes, I have been candid about how painful they can be, but I really want to reassure you that they are a life-saving option. I know a few people who have had abortions, some had similar experiences to me, others carried on their day with very little pain. Either way, being able to *not* have a baby, when you don't want one, should be a human right. Others at twenty-five are more worldly wise, more suited to becoming parents, but I would not have been ready. I also wasn't ready to share this, but I am now. As soon as the hormones dissipated and time passed, I literally never thought about it again. I have no emotional connection to having had an abortion. It feels as routine as going for a cervical screening. It has left no mark on me. The emotional turmoil I suffered was nothing to do with terminating a very early pregnancy, but the myths that women have been fed about our duty, the importance of motherhood, the holiness of conception, that it may never happen again. Had I become a mother then, I truly believe it would have ruined my life. If I can never get pregnant again, I will still be glad I had that abortion. It feels like a lifetime ago. I live in a different place. I am no longer with Z, but I am a mother . . .

It's time for me to tell you about Astrid. In September 2020, Z and I moved into a place of our own, a two-bed flat in Balham with a little garden. It was very modern, not exactly to my taste, but objectively a gorgeous flat. Having spent the first lockdown in a tiny sixth floor flat with no outdoor space, we were determined to make sure that we had access to greenery this time around. I had become obsessed with getting a cat. I had heard someone use the phrase 'having another heartbeat in the house' when I was pregnant and perhaps the turmoil of a pandemic, mixed with the abortion, had made me determined to get more heart-beats into our home. If they weren't going to be human, feline seemed just as good.

'I hate cats,' said Z. 'You can get really cute ones,' I said. 'I must have shown you Mary, Tiffany's British short hair she had when she moved back to the UK?' (Everything in our family has been called Mary, both my maternal and paternal grandmothers, a duck, a rabbit, a cat and now my mum's beloved cockapoo.) 'Cats are evil, I hate cats.' These conversations went on for a while, before I had a stroke of genius. 'What about a really, really small dog? Do you remember Emily's friend Jess's chihuahuas that mum and I looked after. They were sooo cute, look, I'll find a photo.'

We were out for dinner at a family-run Italian on Balham High Road. It was a balmy September evening and I was holding up a picture of two chihuahuas, my phone mere millimetres away from Z's nose, as I did my best Puss in Boots pleading eyes behind my outstretched arm. It was an impromptu dinner. After being locked up for so long I found it easier to coerce Z into spontaneity, because, truthfully, we might not be able to go out tomorrow. We were both sufficiently boozed at this point, my lips purpling in their cracks from the wine, my cheeks flushed as they always did. I was spilling over the edges of myself, bubbling, fizzing, effervescing; laughter or tears alike, threatening to escape me at any given moment; a little too loud, too emotional, too much.

After we'd staggered home, warm and fuzzy from the pasta, wine and tiramisu, I flopped on to the bed and immediately Facetimed my mum. 'Mum, we're getting a dog! Z said we can get a dog, I am *so* excited.' He sauntered in brushing his teeth and gave me a knowing look, which said 'Do you really have to ring your mum right now?' I have a habit of ringing my mum immediately after any emotional situation, from mild amusement to absolute catatonic sadness. I rolled my eyes and focussed back on my mum. 'I've already found the chihuahua I want. I've been speaking to the breeders. Let me send you a video. She's sooo sweet.'

On 4 November, exactly seven months after I flushed the toilet on a potential pregnancy, I went to pay my potential puppy a visit. I was going to meet her and the breeders. I wanted to meet her mum as well and check that everything was above board. I wouldn't get her unless I was absolutely certain. Z said in no uncertain terms that she was to be, in every sense of the word, my dog. I would be the one to pay for her and care for her. That was absolutely fine by me. I was desperate to prove myself as responsible. I had spent too long playing the manic pixie dream girl; the girl who has clothes strewn about the place in the name of creativity; who prefers things to happen to her, rather than making them happen. I ordered *Chihuahuas for Dummies* on Amazon and read it cover to cover. I immersed myself in online forums about small dogs, familiarising myself with the dos and don'ts of dog parenting. I felt more prepared than I have done for anything else in my life.

I got the train to Canterbury, feeling anxiety building in my gut the whole time. What if it was a puppy farm? What if I hadn't researched properly? I had a list of questions to ask the breeder on my phone and I kept scanning the words on the screen, not actually reading them as my mind raced with excitement. At their house, I was greeted by a cacophony of barks, a flurry of fur and the faint smell of urine. They had five adult chihuahuas, all totally different in appearance. One was tiny, apple-headed and blonde, like Paris Hilton's infamous noughties accessory. Another was taller and pointier, more like a shrunken whippet. The parents of my potential pup were larger and long-haired. The father, Roman, had bulging eyes and an impressive plumage; the mother, Zoe, was soft grey with fawn-coloured legs and patches on her chest. They were both tricoloured with lion-like manes and curious eyes.

The puppies were in an open-top crate, falling over each other, grunting and squeaking like little piglets. The one that was marked down for me was the only girl and the fattest. Her belly was bald and rotund, her ears floppy. I could feel tears in my eyes as I fell in love with her on the spot. I even gave her a name: Astrid. Callum, one half of the couple, opened the crate door and the tiny creatures spilled into the living room, charging about after each other. Astrid ambled out behind them. I perched on the couch, watching them.

Zoe jumped up to investigate me. She was delicate, calm and temperamentally unlike any chihuahua I had met before. I stroked her head. Callum's boyfriend handed me Astrid. I cupped her uncertainly in my hands. She was so little. I sat her on my lap, where she flopped between my legs, absentmindedly observing her boisterous brothers as they played on the carpeted floor below. They nibbled at each other's ankles and hid from each other behind the legs of the table before pouncing in mock predatory behaviour. I swear I could hear them laughing.

She was beautiful, with big blue eyes and bluey grey fur. A white stripe neatly parted the middle of her forehead, as though it had been painted on. She was perfect. I was desperate to take her home, but I did my due diligence all the same. I spent forty-five minutes asking questions about the couple's history as breeders, about the health of Astrid's parents and their records. After this unnecessarily long interrogation, I plopped her on the floor. She rolled on to her back, arms outstretched, bald tummy exposed in all its glory. The men laughed, offering her belly rubs. 'She loves this!' they said, knowingly. They weren't wrong. She enjoys at least five belly rub sessions per day. Once I had signed the papers and my precious cargo was stowed away in her carry crate, Callum's boyfriend began to cry. 'We were going to keep her if no one bought her,' he explained. I got a pang of guilt, as is my disposition. I solemnly gestured handing her back. They laughed, waved me away and with sniffly noses ushered me to their car to drop me back at the station.

I had been on the waiting list for various adoption services in London for months prior, but with the caveat that I wanted a young, small dog. With adoption it's hard to be prescriptive, but living in a London flat meant I simply didn't have the space for a bigger dog and, not having grown up with dogs, I felt nervous about adopting one that might need an experienced owner. Ideally a puppy that I could train would make me feel comfortable. When nothing became available, I started speaking to breeders. Before I got Astrid, I had wondered about how my audience would receive me buying a puppy. I had seen others getting a lot of flak for not adopting and I wasn't sure I wanted to deal with that. I also felt a level of responsibility in that if I wasn't going to adopt, was I then going to influence a whole cohort of people to buy? That didn't sit well with me either.

A lot of influencers who were getting 'lockdown dogs' were using them as steadfast parts of their content. I knew I wanted Astrid. I knew I was ready for her, but I couldn't figure out how sharing her would work. I wouldn't post a child, I reasoned, because they couldn't consent to it. What if she started getting gifted things? Or companies wanted to advertise with her? I would be posting her for content and that wasn't why I was getting her. She was my extra heartbeat in the house, not an extra accessory for content.

When I got home, I sat her on a puppy pad in the middle of the living room and thought, 'What the fuck have I done?' I played her calming music and gave her some food and water. I put my hoody that I had been wearing on the floor and she immediately went to it, curled up in a ball and fell asleep. She still has that hoody in her crate today. I fell in love with the name Astrid after reading *Crazy Rich Asians*, in which Astrid is the cousin of the love interest: she's beautiful, loyal and kind. Her character imbued the name with so many positive attributes and it suits my Astrid perfectly. I got full custody after Z and I broke up. She is, always was and always will be *my* dog.

It felt strange not to share her at first, and then soon it became the easiest thing in the world. I love her more than anything I have ever loved. I spend pretty much every waking moment with her. It feels weird telling you all about her now. If I am being totally truthful, one of the main reasons I didn't share her initially was exactly because the climate online had become quite hostile. People were getting 'cancelled' for eating the wrong hummus. I don't really believe that being cancelled has material repercussions, but an onslaught of judgement and hate is painful no matter what. Truthfully, I felt like I couldn't risk putting myself through it. I didn't feel strong enough.

I had been through an experience before where people got angry at me for not acknowledging my thin privilege on a post about having overcome an unhealthy relationship with exercise. And although I understood where these people were coming from – that a lot of the messages were emotional and more about them than me – I struggled with it so much I almost had a break-down. Having so many people tell you you're a terrible human, when perhaps your crime isn't really one worth that much vitriol, is hard. In part because of the content of my podcast, I was being held to a high moral stand-ard, one that at times felt impossible to meet. I knew there was the risk that people would be disappointed or angry or see me as a bad person for not adopting. My friends obviously found this hilarious and ridiculous, but also sadly telling. 'You can't think like this, Nones. It's your life!' It was the beginning of me opening the channel to others' perceptions of me, the one that allowed comments on gossip websites to change how I acted and viewed myself. For what it's worth, I do think it is the better choice to adopt and, having been a dog-parent for over two years, I would feel competent enough to do so now. But I also feel that it seems trivial to worry about other people's judgements of my choices and would share her if I got her today.

I thought I would probably share her after a few months, once I was more settled with her and had fig-ured out how to respond to criticism, but as time went on I realised I loved having her to myself. Why did any-one need to know, anyway? Having been online for so much of my adult life, and at points having felt so over-exposed, having something that was mine, wholly mine, has been a lifeline. She isn't an accessory, or content, she's basically my daughter. She goes by many names, coined by myself, my friends and family: Astrid, the Baby, the Mythical Magical Creature, the Pixie and Baby Yoda. I even have a tiny tattoo of the Mandalorian on the inside of my right forearm. If you see me in the park with her, please do say hi. She doesn't bite. Ask any of my friends, she's the best chihuahua in the world.

She was also the punctuation mark, the opening chapter, of a new beginning for me. There had come a turning point when my identity became messily enmeshed with social media. I felt responsible for good press about the platforms, but was tired of having to constantly field jibes about swipe up links, discount codes and boyfriends of Instagram. I was defensive of the industry and fed up of my work being willfully misunderstood. It became so all-consuming that I felt as though any negativity about social media as a whole was about me, too. I was doing everything I could to be a *good* influence, but no matter how hard I tried, I had become jaded and feared that I couldn't escape the feeling of being judged.

That summer, sat around a gorgeous farmhouse table, drinking Italian wine and eating a variety of local cheeses, my friends and I embarked on a round of the 'name on the head game', which I'll happily instigate at any available moment. I am a stickler for organised fun, particularly in the form of after-dinner games. Somehow, with Marilyn Monroe, Jemima Puddleduck and other various pop-culture characters scribbled on torn paper stuck to our foreheads, the conversation turned to social media. The discussion quickly became heated. 'It's just bad for your mental health full stop,' came one comment. 'It gives people eating disorders,' came another. I felt the hairs on the back of my neck stand up, my cheeks flush with shame and my smile tighten in a way that I'm sure looked more like a grimace. When I heard the tenth iteration of 'Social media is bad,' my brain translated it into 'You're a bad person.' I tried to join the debate in defence of the platforms, with examples of the body positivity movement, of online organising turning into grass roots activism, of social-issues education for the privileged and community building for the marginalised. But I was warm and heady from the wine, unable to provide sufficient evidence to the group, overwhelmed by how emotional and attacking this felt when it wasn't about me at all. I found myself unable to carry on the conversation. The tension became too much and I took myself away to my room where I stewed, unable to understand why I felt so hurt and attacked.

Unusually this didn't go away and what should've been a lighthearted debate turned into a depressive episode for me, unlike anything I had experienced since university. When I got back to London, I spent days on the sofa, feeling insane. I was confused by how my body and mind were reacting to words and ideas that were commonplace. I guess it hurt because it mattered to me that people saw my industry as I saw it. I knew the wider media minimised and was callous about influencers, but these people knew me, knew my work. I felt like all my insecurities were laid out on the table alongside the antipasti to be dissected, masticated and eventually burnt up by stomach acid.

This was just a trigger point, but it pushed me to take a step. I called Grace, who always, without fail, answers the phone when I need her. She has so much patience and had always spoken to me so candidly, naturally and, well, gracefully about mental health. She assured me that I wasn't insane, that I had been telling her for a while that I was struggling and that for some unfortunate reason my root issue had been prodded and poked under the Tuscan sun. 'Why don't you try therapy?' she offered. A friend had previously told me about psychologytoday. com, where you can search for therapists in your area and find one that looks suitable for whatever it is you need to work through, and how you want to approach it. I sent out various enquiries to therapists who I thought I might click with, eventually landing on Claire who lived a fifteen-minute walk away from my flat. I agonised over what to wear, deciding on off-white, low-rise baggy jeans, with my new teal-blue toed, tan leather cowboy boots, a white Peter Pan collar shirt, charity shop Aquascutum trench coat and sunglasses. I think I thought the more time I invested in my outfit the less time I would have to panic about what I was about to do.

It was a balmy October day, my upper lip and forehead glistened in the unseasonal warmth, and my boots rubbed uncomfortably at my heels as I marched uncertainly towards my first session. I had no idea what it would be like, only that words, emotions and memories were brimming at the edges of my very being. The moment I sat down on the sofa, paragraphs fell out of my mouth without punctuation. I barely remember coming up for breath, only noticing the wetness of my cheeks as I finally paused and searched the face of my therapist for answers. She took a deep breath and said, 'I am so glad you came in today.' The specifics of what I spoke about in therapy aren't something I plan on disclosing, but like every other human being alive I have moments from my past that have lodged themselves into my bones, burrowing away deep into the crevices of my skull, floating idly along the rivers of my veins and, unbeknownst to me, hacking my system from time to time.

Because I hadn't fallen into addiction, was in a healthy relationship, and had an objectively exciting and promising career path, good friendships and all the other things I thought made a stable person, I assumed I had dealt with all the things that had come up – by burying them. Reader, I hadn't dealt with any of it, not at all. I had managed to put a stopper in it, which for the most part contained it. The stopper had got tighter and tighter as the years went on, but whenever I was shaken or felt attacked, or as though I was being ridiculed, I wouldn't always be able to stop it from bubbling up to the surface and escaping me in moments as inconsequential as an after-dinner debate. What I did not speak about was my career or that conversation in Italy. That was, as it turned out, completely irrelevant.

At university I had felt less in control. I would slip in and out of down periods. They always seemed to come from interactions where I felt misunderstood or otherwise exposed. I never told anyone. It terrified me that my mood could plummet so quickly. At points I had become obsessed with the idea that something was very wrong with me, because what was I so afraid of people seeing in me? Why did I have so much self-doubt about the essence of who I was? Why was it so grounding to create a page that visibly detailed my character, my likes and dislikes, my identity?

Therapy at first was an offloading project. The hour would end before I had even finished expunging the memories that I didn't know held so much power over me. A few months in, I came home from a session and cried for an entire day. I cried so much it felt like I had been exorcised. I was exhausted, spent and, like a storm passing, as the tears dried up it felt like a little light was starting to peek through the dark clouds hanging above my head. After seeing my therapist for over a year and talking for an hour each week, we parted ways in early 2022. I haven't had any significant mental health wobbles since. I hadn't even realised that the problems I had been having internally were due to unresolved childhood experiences, let alone that they could be resolved. If you need motivation to seek out therapy, please let this be it. Whilst I know the waiting lists can be long on the NHS and private therapy is expensive, you can search IAPT for NHS services or check psychologytoday.com for therapists near you. Some offer sliding scale prices to suit your income. There is no shame in speaking to someone. Not everyone suffers from mental illness, but everyone has mental health and, just like going to the gym for your body, it's important to look after your brain, too.

Appropriately enough, in May 2021 I was honoured to be invited to talk at the Royal College of Psychiatrists' international congress, where the topic was social media and mental health in young people. Nikki, a medical student who at the time was writing for the *British Medical Journal*, is a follower of mine. She reached out via DMs to ask if I would be interested in offering a different perspective on the ways we can harness social media for good. She felt some of the doctors speaking on the panel might not use social media in the same way their prospective patients do, and so it would be fruitful to broaden the discussion with insights from someone who understood it from the inside.

I was asked to deliver a twenty-minute talk, speaking as someone with the lived experience of both working as influencer and using the platforms as a consumer. Feeling like I had to bring more than anecdotes to the table, I gathered some statistics from my audience prior to giving the talk. I did a poll asking whether they believed social media had a net-positive or net-negative impact on their mental health. Most of my Instagram audience are eighteen- to thirty-five-year-old women living in the UK, but participants could tick different age brackets for some of the questions. I had around twelve thousand people answering and sixty-eight percent of those responded that they believed social media had a net-negative impact on their mental health. Whilst not shocking, it was still a damning result, one that didn't sit well with me for obvious reasons. I wanted to delve deeper, so I asked some follow-up questions. The overwhelming recurring answer for why people found it negative was due to comparison: comparing lives, bodies, relationships, wealth, success, fear of missing out and feeling like a failure. I wasn't surprised by these answers, but I did start to wonder if maybe the issue was the platforms themselves and the way they have been created, rather than us being responsible for the way that we use them. So, I put forward two statements on my stories and asked people to vote for the one which they agreed with most. The first was:

Social media is problematic because of the culture in which it has been created and coded. Because we live in a systemically racist, ableist, fatphobic, homophobic, transphobic society, the platforms algorithmically encourage those same problems that exist within society.

The second was:

Social media is inherently bad. No matter which way you format it, we simply cannot cope with being exposed to this many people. It's never going to be able to be safeguarded and it is just inherently damaging.

This time there was a sixty-forty split in favour of the first statement – that social media in of itself is not inherently evil, but that its fundamental composition is flawed. What made sense to me, too, is that from an evolutionary point of view humans are designed to live in communities of around one hundred and fifty people. We simply wouldn't have had access to so many different people of disparate backgrounds. We shouldn't be able to compare ourselves to hundreds of people per minute, and as Rutger Bregman notes, 'People are social animals, but we have a fatal flaw: we feel more affinity for those who are most like us.'[6] So, comparing ourselves to people who are wealthier than us, or what we perceive as more beautiful, or happier, can, of course, cause us discomfort. Then again, we aren't living in the past. Capitalism means we are always seeking more ways to optimise both ourselves and our lives, and because of that ideological drive, aspirational content can also be inspirational and enjoyable for some.

---

[6] *Human kind*, Rutger Bregman, Bloomsbury, 2020.

People who use it for escapism, a look into the lives of people who live in a completely different way to them, may not find it harmful. But for a lot of people, as we all know, constantly looking at other people's 'highlight reels' can cause great dissatisfaction and insecurity about their own life. What's pertinent is figuring out the boundaries that each person needs, what each individual will benefit from taking away from these platforms, and which accounts aren't benefitting them that they should unfollow. Because there are undoubtedly good parts.

The responses that came up for the positive aspects of social media were creativity, learning, education, community, friendship building, work opportunities, inspiration (in areas from interior design and styling to exercise and ways to cope with mental health struggles). Perhaps because I am on these platforms so much myself, and have at times felt a certain way, I have already done my own safeguarding. Over the years I have created boundaries around who and what I follow, as well as how much and what I share, although there is undoubtedly privilege in being able to curate your feed. For one thing, I'm twenty-nine as opposed to eighteen or younger. I know myself well enough to recognise when something is a projection of my own insecurities that I can interrogate and hopefully overcome, or otherwise be aware when something simply doesn't serve me. A quote that I always go back to is from Daisy Buchanan's memoir *The Sisterhood*, where she discusses the way that women especially are conditioned to compete with each other. She quotes Amy Poehler's 'Good for her, not for me' and goes on to say this 'means good for Emily Ratajkowski, in her spaghetti! Her work has nothing to do with yours.' This is easier said than done, because, and perhaps most importantly, I know what it takes to make a feed a feed.

As a creator I am aware of the smoke and mirrors. I know what goes into creating a certain type of photo, as well as being able to intuit the negative space that doesn't make it online. And then even when it does, it's still a curated reality. I know what goes on behind the lens. I can zoom out in my mind's eye and imagine the pile of dirty laundry next to the glamorous mirror selfie of my favourite style guru, expertly cropped out. I know just how hard that fitness influencer has worked to look a certain way from when I did bodybuilding and am grateful to know that I am happy with how I use my time, which means I won't necessarily look like her. Often, it's the mystery and mystique of something that makes us feel self-doubt, whereas once we understand how something works it's much easier to make an informed decision, rather than feeling locked out. I am lucky in that respect. The majority of influencers curate a feed that is designed to be aspirational: the beauty of the thing is often the point of it. Much like a supermodel whose job it is to work out three times a day and maintain a certain physique, perfect skin and hair, so, too, is it the job of the influencer to put a pro-verbial rose tint over the lives they choose to share.

However, constantly viewing content that deviates from what we can personally achieve, or envision for ourselves, can indeed be a bad thing. Of course, it's difficult to control and manage everything we take in, with the onus on the consumer, and it would be much better if the platforms themselves could prioritise each individual's mental health. There's an interesting dichotomy, whereby the negatives of social media amplify the problems that exist in day-to-day life, due to how these platforms are coded. But at the same time, we see a huge, often productive, resistance coming from the users of those same platforms.

For example, model and activist Nyome Nicholas-Williams (@curvynyome) received an apology from Instagram, after they took down a photo of her shot by photographer Alex Cameron. 'Millions of pictures of very naked, skinny white women can be found on Instagram every day, but a fat Black woman celebrating her body is banned? I feel like I'm being silenced,' she told the *Observer*.[7] In the same article, Cameron said that the images being removed of Nyome weren't only similar to photographs she had taken of white women, which never got flagged or taken down, but they were less revealing than a lot of them, too. After encouraging their followers to share the images far and wide with the hashtag #IWantToSeeNyome, they wrote to

---

[7] 'Instagram "censorship" of black model's photo reignites claims of race bias', Nosheen Iqbal, *Observer*, August 2020.

the head of Instagram Adam Mosseri. He emailed Nyome to apologise and tweeted, 'We stand in solidarity with the Black community. But that's not enough. Words are not enough. That's why we're committed to looking at the ways our policies, tools, and processes impact Black people and other underrepresented groups on Instagram.'

As individuals we're vulnerable to such vast digital giants, but for communities, or coalition building, especially for social justice movements, social media has been instrumental. As I mentioned at that dinner in Tuscany, if we look at things like the body positive movement, which is not something I'd heard of as a young girl, nowadays vast swathes of young people not only know what body positivity is, but also what the roots of it are, what the fat liberation movement is and how it was started. The push from activists, campaigns and individuals alike not only adjusts the climate online, but offline, too. With digital overtaking print, traditional media has to listen to those who garner attention online, even if it is just to save their own industry, the effect is the same, and that is giving more space to those who are marginalised. This is not happening frequently enough or being executed perfectly, but it is happening.

If only we were taught from a very young age that social media is like alcohol: you don't drink it all day long, but you can enjoy it in moderation, perhaps as you watch your favourite show in the evening or during a break from work. Every now and then it is absolutely fine, good for you, even, content dependent. Obviously, some people will have an unhealthy relationship with it, but quite a lot of people might be able to find joy in it. The problem is, the age at which people are being introduced to social media is getting younger and younger, with not enough safeguarding or education around its dangers and how addictive it is. However, I truly believe that if people are taught how to manage their social media on their own, we might figure out how to harness all of those incredible aspects of social media: creativity, learning, education, community friendship building, opportunities. I wish I had said all this so eloquently at that dinner.

Chapter 7

THE LIGHT OF the late morning winter sun snaked along the walls and danced across the fireplace, brightening the empty space that was my new home. I exhaled. I felt free. It was as though I had been under water all that time, and now I could finally come up for air, see things more clearly. I unpacked my multicoloured vases, sorted through my antique ornaments and table books, and placed them on the mantelpiece. As I did so, my eyes started to prick with tears. I wasn't sad, I was relieved. When I saw the high ceilings, original floorboards and old fixtures of this place, I knew it felt like home. All the tiles in the bathroom were cracked, the doors unpainted, still bare wood, and the kitchen falling apart, but it was a beautifully imperfect blank canvas and it was to be all mine. I signed the lease for a year. I decorated it slowly and methodically, relishing in making the space wholly me in every way. I spent hours painstakingly trawling websites for second-hand furniture, adamant I wouldn't buy anything new. I ventured to local antique shops and bought glass ashtrays and odd little knickknacks. Colour and patterns and candles and glass and JOY. I bought myself fresh flowers every week, exercised every morning and danced almost every evening.

I walked Astrid, I wrote, I did stand-up and I painted. For the first time since I had created it, I didn't prioritise my Instagram. I started to learn to care less. I started paying attention to the real world, rather than the histrionics of social media. I went on a solo trip to Lisbon where I ate *pastéis de nata*, drank wine by the glass at bars on my own and wrote from a little nook in the garden of my Airbnb. I saw my friends more than I had ever done in the last four years. I didn't miss a single social event. I took up netball. I drank more spicy margaritas than is sensible. I hosted dinner parties and BBQs and drinks. I went on dates. I kissed men in bars and chatted to them in fancy restaurants. I spoke to them on apps and I met them at parties. I was resolute in one thing: I was going to stay single. I was going to *Eat, Pray, Love* minus the praying. Maybe *Eat, Party, Love*?

My last relationship had been too regimented, too serious, too certain in its constitution; a constitution which ultimately, whilst never toxic nor unhealthy, simply wasn't for me. In an episode of *Sentimental*

Garbage, Dolly Alderton says, 'Being swallowed up by a relationship and a man's identity . . . it's so instinctive and it's so culturally conditioned with women to do it.' So much of who I thought I was supposed to be was tied up in that relationship; tied up in the timelines that society had neatly set out.

Suddenly, I felt ten years younger. It was 2022 and I was newly single, newly therapised and about to embark on a fresh, unchartered chapter. Most of my early twenties had been about my career, about constantly reinventing the wheel, reinventing myself and continuously having to prove myself – so much so that I hadn't ever really acknowledged before just how much it had taken for me to sustain being self-employed straight out of uni, in a precarious industry, with no clue what I was doing, for all this time. I hadn't built a multi-million-pound empire, created my own brand or grown my account (despite getting new followers, I lost just as many), but I had still done it. I had turned being an influencer into a real job.

I got very lucky, that's for sure, but I had also spent so long allowing myself to be defined by other people's ideas of me, at the mercy of other people's routines, in fear of strangers' projections. This year, I decided, was to be all about exploration. I was to gather everything I had learnt about the world and myself and figure it all out, once and for all.

I filled my life with colour. I wore outrageous outfits and experimented with make-up. I felt like I was

Carrie Bradshaw, complete with storing clothes in my crockery cupboard and taking up smoking again for a bit. I hadn't been a smoker since my last year of uni, but it was like I was taking advantage of every freedom available to me. I was recalibrating, resetting, being irresponsible, reckless, but I was doing it on purpose. I was letting go, fucking around and finding out.

After almost seven years of building a profile, of endlessly plugging away at this venture that I had now come to see as my career, I suddenly felt tired. I had established a community which not only was I grateful for, but which I had truly grown to love as a collective. The professional aspect aside, the whole reason I was able to, wanted to, carry on in times of uncertainty was because of my followers. Most of my adult life had been shared with these people and, for the most part, up until more recently, this had been a heartening thing. Every time I met any of my audience in real life, I felt honoured that these women supported me. My book clubs are the best example of this, when I would get to spend hours chatting and learning from people who were so absorbing, remarkable and funny. I would come away from the evening thinking that any of them could do what I do, perhaps even better than I do. I felt a duty to show up, no matter how menial it seemed to the disbelievers. These women had given me so much more than my career; they had given me confidence, ideas and inspiration.

But what being chronically online also teaches you is to be pre-emptive to the point of paralysis. Everything you do and say online can and will be used against you in the court of the internet, with a jury made up of your followers, trolls, friends and family alike. It can feel like you're one misstep away from a Russian doll of hot takes collapsing in on each other, eating themselves, dissolving into kindling for the next forest fire. You must either be able to build up skin thick enough to rise up out of the ashes, attempt (fruitlessly) to please everyone or, eventually, become mute. I have tried each option and it seems a combination of the three works best: Knowing when to shut up, when to apologise and when to batten down the hatches of your emotions.

Some influencers seem to make themselves deliberately unlikeable to appear authentic – as the old adage goes 'the truth hurts' – and oxymoronically cruelty can sometimes be the key to a loyal fanbase. Contrarians, usually men, build entire careers from telling people to fuck off, offering hard-to-swallow takes and stirring the proverbial pot of internet discourse. Authenticity has become the ultimate badge of honour and, in a society that is ever more sceptical of social media, meanness can act as a misleading signifier of truth-telling. This is not something I could ever do, no matter how provocative or profitable it may be. I still, deep down, just really want everyone to like me. It's very hard to get out of the habit of caring what people think. We are trained to do it from a very young age and when your career somewhat depends on your likeability, it can make it even tougher to take criticism with a pinch of salt. And even if I wanted to, as Shona wrote on her stories recently, 'If women used this tactic we would be absolutely (metaphorically) slaughtered for this kind of behaviour. Gender norms accept men being more polarising.' I didn't want to polarise, I knew that much, but I also didn't know what I did want to post or say.

I wasn't sure I could keep up anymore. Creators are more creative than ever, the platforms are so satiated and I knew I was falling behind. This reminded me of that *New York Times* piece on influencer burnout, which recalled YouTuber Olga Kay telling *Fast Company* in 2014 'If you slow down, you might disappear.'[8] I watched as friends migrated to TikTok, adapting to the new platform with ease, building new streams of content and revenue, but another platform felt like a daunting and overwhelming prospect. I didn't know what else I had left to give. I didn't know if I wanted to do this anymore. A quote kept popping into my mind: 'Whatever you feed, grows.' If I kept watering the proverbial garden of my social media, it would flourish, but I wasn't sure that was what I wanted – not entirely, not anymore.

My friend Chloe Plumstead, who is also an influencer (and who I greatly admire), posted this on her stories:

---

[8] 'Young Creators are Burning Out and Breaking Down', Taylor Lorenz, *New York Times*, June 2021.

I haven't been filming, writing or taking many photos recently. I think a part of that comes from sincerely being sick of looking at my own face or my own home or spending too much time with my own thoughts, and believing that every idea or thought is a bag of shit but knowing this blip will pass. But I do also feel restless with work. I've been doing the same thing for some time now and I have undeniable itchy feet, thinking about what could be next for me and trying to discern what feels right (spoiler: nothing, I am very confused and I feel like I'm floating in liminal space).

You know when you have a moment where you're suddenly confronted with the question of: what the hell am I doing with my life? And then you start to panic (albeit quietly) and explore every possible avenue of change, hoping for some kind of a-ha moment that will bring purpose and if not fulfilment, at least a kind of grounding, the kind of reinforcement that tells you you're not wasting your time.

With growing intensity I have found myself thinking, what the fuck am I doing at nearly 29 years old, taking videos of my outfits? Or using stories like my own personal private public journal? You know when you have that kind of out-of-body, seeing-yourself-through-the-eyes-of-others experience and it doesn't really align with how you see yourself (or who you *want* to be) and you know it's a 'growth moment' (ew) and change isn't terrible but also no? I want to have all the answers and not have to go through this uncomfortable in-between bit.

Anyway I'm not entirely sure that any of this is making sense which is why I haven't been clogging up your feed with the inane ramblings of a quarter life crisis which is relentlessly pushing on. Who am I?

What do I want? What the hell am I doing? Do I like olives now? NOTHING MAKES SENSE.

Those words resonated with me so much. What did I have left to share? I was exercising regularly, so perhaps I could've gone back to fitness content? But I had worked so hard to step away from that world. Even though I loved fashion, what could I provide for my audience? I had shirked fast fashion, and mostly bought clothes from charity shops. I watched younger TikTokkers creating style videos and loved seeing them put together pieces from Depop and Ebay, but I knew that would entail hours spent buying clothes, creating video content of me trying on outfits and then what? It wouldn't give me the satisfaction I desired, plus I barely had enough space for the clothes I already owned. Without clothes that were shoppable for my audience, sharing my style seemed sort of fruitless. I had cordoned off lots of my private life, not wanting the focus to be on my romantic relationships, and I was embarking on doing stand-up, but I wanted to figure this out on a real stage, not in online sketches. What then, was left for me to influence? It felt like I was finally losing my spot in the rat race. What remained to be said? How many corners of myself could I successfully mine before all that was left for me was my shell? I realised I had nothing left to share precisely because I had become so online that I wasn't in and of the world anymore. I needed time away to think, reassess, evolve.

Comedy turned out to be one of the best salves for my previously skittish fear of saying or doing the wrong thing at any given moment. I would constantly be on edge, worried I would be caught out, even when I hadn't done anything, as though the streets were paved with banana skins and booby traps. Up on stage, I could say anything, it seemed. I didn't have to appear respectable, relatable or responsible. In fact, no one expected anything from me at all. If anything, people probably expected me to be bad, but if I was, only the people in the room knew. If I was great, the same was true. This was liberating. I became more brazen with the stories I told, scouring the events from my year of freedom for jokes and anecdotes. I took the piss out of myself. I stopped taking everything so seriously.

However, every now and then I would get a rush of fear and guilt about not posting any useful content on my Instagram. I was starting to lose followers and, whilst stand-up comedy, painting and writing were giving me something I hadn't had for years – a space to hone a craft in private, over a long period of time – they weren't going to get me ads, which had for a long while, since I stopped the podcast, been my sole source of income. I had the first instalment of the advance from my book, some savings and intermittent income from ads to tide me over, but without my podcast and consistent revenue from brand sponsorship I would soon have less money than I had done for a while, and at the same time my rent had basically doubled due to living alone. The gossips were gossiping away, though, and I didn't have the energy to prove anything to them, or to give them anything, so I turned up in the most basic way: I just shared all the fun I was having.

My audience were interested in my new single status, frequently questioning how I was finding being single 'at twenty-eight'. This amused me, as often these messages were accompanied with a hint of concern. 'Twenty-eight is YOUNG,' I wrote on my stories, accompanied by a picture of me sticking my tongue out, which is some sort of pose disease I can't overcome. But it got me thinking about how much women are conditioned to panic as we approach thirty. How none of my single male friends seem to be doing calculations around how quickly they ought to meet a partner to have a baby by thirty-two. I considered my conversations with friends in the pub, which were in equal parts about who we had snogged the night before and whether or not we wanted to get married, or move out of London, or freeze our eggs. This was new and sudden. I wanted to know if everyone was feeling this pressure to count their chickens before the eggs had hatched, or more aptly worrying about how many eggs we had before we even knew if we even wanted any chickens in the first place. I didn't know if I was fertile, but I knew this was fertile ground for a discussion about the timelines of our life and how much we are subconsciously influenced by the traditional and sometimes archaic timelines encouraged by society. I wanted to hear from people who had done things on their own terms; who hadn't necessarily had things go to plan, but had still worked stuff out. I decided I was going to relaunch my podcast as *Adulting 2.0: Timelines* and do exactly that.

In December 2021 I booked myself a solo trip to Positano for the following May. I stayed in a hotel where everyone was on their honeymoon. I sat by the pool drinking iced oat lattes, writing this book and watching snoozing couples hold hands across sunbeds. I climbed hundreds of stairs to find family-run restaurants with the best seafood pasta. I went to cocktail bars on my own, once making friends with a newly engaged couple and ending up in the only club in the village, dancing with them and a group of gay men who I made friends with that night, too. I took myself for three-course lunches, always followed by a tiramisu. I wrote.

On the last Saturday of the trip, I asked a guy I had been dating casually, on and off, if he wanted to fly out for the weekend. I was in my 'treating myself' era. It was my Samantha Jones moment. I went on a financially irresponsible spree in the town and bought a new dress, strappy heels and a pashmina. The latter I will never wear again. It really only made sense on the Amalfi Coast. He arrived that evening. We ate oysters, drank champagne and chatted under the stars, listening to the gentle lapping of the waves. Girlies, it was truly the most romantic thing ever.

Three weeks later, I went to Ibiza with Steph, Poppie and our other best friend Izzy. None of us had ever been there before and we weren't sure what to expect, but we had booked a hefty nine nights and we decided we'd figure it out once we had arrived. The first night we went to a local restaurant. It wasn't going to be a late one, we'd only just landed and we wouldn't be eating until 9pm, so dinner and drinks then bed was the plan. The restaurant sat on a beach overlooking the sea, and across the water you could see the lights and life of the main strip. After stuffing ourselves with the best the Balearics had to offer, Poppie looked up from her phone. 'Guys, I have been speaking to this guy for a bit on this dating app and he wants to know if we want to go to Pacha?'

Twenty minutes and a chaotic turn around in our Airbnb later, we're in a cab, wearing a mismatch of each other's clothes, after trying to figure out the perfect look for the club. We get there and it turns out 'this guy' is best friends with Robin Schulz, who is headlining. We are instructed to head into the private area just behind the DJ booth. We look out on to the throngs of people, and then we look at each other and laugh in disbelief. We dance until the early hours and when the club closes we look on the map for a beach. There's one not too far away. We get to the water, strip off our clothes and dive into the ocean butt-naked. Everything about the last twelve hours feels like it was straight out of a movie. We paddle around in the water, floating idly on our backs, letting the early morning sun warm our faces and bare bodies, before we get dressed and head back.

Somehow, this wasn't the peak of our trip. Every single day, good fortune found us. We laughed all day by the pool, eating copious amounts of chips and pizza, before heading out to dinner, dressed to the nines. Hours later we'd find ourselves two-stepping in our maxi-dresses, heels in our hands, cares nowhere to be seen. One evening after dinner we got matching tattoos that read 'love you forever' and a little red heart on our wrist. On the last day, we got another, an upside-down horseshoe, because every single day in Ibiza we couldn't stop saying, 'We're the luckiest girls in the world.' It felt like after the pandemic, various break-ups and life changes and the angst of our earlier twenties, this, twenty-eight, was a great age. Life was only going to get better. Save for Steph, we were all single. When we spoke about Ibiza, we imagined it to be our 'Hot Girl Summer'. We'd envisioned mini summer romances, stolen kisses in packed rooms and wandering hands at sunset. Instead, we spent the whole trip falling in love with each other.

Throughout my career, there have been lots of things that worked, but even more that didn't. Alongside writing this book, I was strategising for my first ever brand – a sustainable jewellery brand. The only material to be used was recycled nine-carat gold, so that it would never tarnish like plated products and would hopefully be at a similar price point to H. Samuel and Argos when they did nine carat products, but with a fresher look. I was going to call it *Olive and Only* – *Olive* after my mum, as some of the designs were based on her old pieces that she had handed down to me, and *only* because it was the only jewellery you would need, as it would never tarnish and you could pass it down through the generations. This would have been momentous for me had I managed to pull it off, only the fulfilment company I was working with went bust a year into the making.

I was also set to host a new podcast that was to be pitched as a Spotify Original, where I would interview established comedians about how they got to where they are today. Only, due to scheduling issues and various other barriers, this also fell through. At the beginning of the year, I had envisioned those three events as defining my 2022, but things don't always go to plan, which I have found out can, a lot of the time, work in your favour. Sometimes you have to trust the timing of your life.

Often the reason people follow influencers is for pure unadulterated voyeurism, a window into the world of celebrity, events and exclusivity. We are the middle(wo)men, granted access to the secret life of actors, models and socialites. It means that the gap between 'normal' civilian and celebrity is bridged, narrowed ever so slightly. Gone are the days of mystery, now anyone with an iPhone can be paparazzi and everyone wants to know everyone's business. Where celebrities previously had no agency over how the media portrayed them, social media has allowed them to voice their comebacks, to take to Twitter to disavow an invariably awful article from the *Daily Mail*, or quash bullshit rumours. It has never been easier to advocate for yourself online, but it has also never been harder to evade public shaming and cruelty.

It's difficult, because I speak from a place of immense privilege, not just systemically, but the fact that I have, in my own small way, made it. I have managed to monetise my life in a way that affords me a well-above average standard of living, lifestyle and freedom. So often I just shut up, because I often do feel like the luckiest woman in the world, like I have won the jackpot – which in many ways I have – even though my career was built over seven years, rather than one day, the risk that it could disappear overnight is always there.

I recently read *Tomorrow, and Tomorrow, and Tomorrow* by Gabrielle Zevin, in which the narrator says, 'There is a time for any fledgling artist where one's taste exceeds one's abilities. The only way to get through this period is to make things anyway.' And that is what I did. I made things, I created and I did it all, for the first time in a long time, in private. I realised, with some relief, as I ate into my now nominal savings with my flat and my trips to Italy and Spain, that as much as I want to be financially stable and successful, the promise of riches alone isn't enough to motivate me to keep going. I must feel useful; feel like I believe in the work I am doing. I don't mind showing up if I am proud of it, but I had lost sight of the point of it all.

I actually have no great plans to become a billionaire or build a multi-million-pound empire. My dreams and aspirations on that scale are much more modest. I simply want a career and life that I find fulfilling, emotionally satiating and intellectually stimulating. Perhaps that is the biggest dream of all. At twenty-eight, I have been a fitness influencer, online coach, personal trainer, podcaster, quasi-journalist, lifestyle influencer, sustainable fashion influencer, activist (albeit briefly), stand-up comedian and, now, author. There are hundreds, if not thousands, if not tens of thousands of creators out there who are much more intelligent and creative, less privileged and harder working than me, many of whom will never get their big break. In 2021 I believed I had been given mine in the form of this book deal, something I could've only ever have dreamt of. Being an influencer is certainly a facet of my work and it might be the most profitable financially, but it is also a springboard that allows me to try out different avenues and figure out exactly what it is that I want to do with my life. I think that is the greatest privilege and it's one that I wish was afforded to everyone.

Afterword

My ETERNAL QUEST has always been to find myself and, over the last seven years, I not only achieved that, but I did so publicly and turned it into a career, with my audience and strangers having a right of reply. Through being an influencer, I have learned a lot, not only about who I am, but about what the world at large thinks of me and people like me.

Throughout this book I have referred to my privilege quite a lot. Maybe that was boring to read; maybe it ceases to make sense the twelfth time. The truth is, as interesting as my journey to becoming an influencer is (at least I hope it is), it is not singular. Many first-generation influencers share something in common: our class. I've never had an allowance, I don't have a trust fund or any form of inheritance to fall back on if this all goes tits up and I have been self-sufficient throughout this unconventional career. But in terms of getting to this point of financial independence, whilst it felt tumultuous at times, when I zoom out I see I have had it tremendously easy. Yes, I do believe that platforms like Instagram and YouTube are more of a meritocracy than some traditional career paths, but it is still people who look and sound like me who manage to navigate to success with greater ease.

I felt a huge level of guilt around this. I struggled to write this book, not because I dislike writing or don't believe in what I am saying, but because on my way to reaching a level of success that afforded me a book deal in the first place I came to really grapple with how I viewed my place in the world. The current conversation around nepo-babies is not dissimilar, and people are understandably becoming less and less tolerant of the invisible advantages that serve those who are already benefiting from our unfair society. On the other hand, conversations around privilege can sometimes be problematic, too. I recently saw a TikTok where a woman privilege-checked a man giving advice on where best to park if you're sleeping in your car by saying some people don't even have a car to sleep in and he should check his privilege. Her follow-up video revealed that she didn't appear to need to sleep in a car, as it was filmed from what looked like the inside of her home.

Either way, I understand the outrage. I recognise that things cannot carry on as they are, cannot keep worsening as they are. With the climate crisis, the cost-of-living crisis, the constant and needed strike action, we are living through a period of huge socio-political unrest. Whilst some people may continue to find joy in the aspirational lives of others online, I can totally appreciate people are experiencing a huge sense of disenfranchisement with the content that used to perform really well years ago. My coming-of-age story has been central to my work in an oddly cannibalistic way, but in writing this book I feel I have closed the lid on this chapter and am ready for the next. I don't know exactly what this looks like yet, or how I can create something functional out of the futile privilege-guilt that I do still carry around with me, but I hope I can find a way to use my influence for good in what-ever way that manifests itself, for however long I have the power.

Outside of my sometimes-all-consuming career, in the parts that I don't share on my Instagram, I am enjoying my little flat, my friendships, my time with Astrid and the bliss of a new romantic relationship. As the wheels of the plane hit the tarmac in London and I was back on home soil after nine perfect days in Ibiza, my first thought was how excited I was to see Astrid. And secondly, with a little flutter in my stomach, the person who had helped me out and collected her from her dog-sitter earlier that day. I met him on Hinge. Let's call him J. He's the one who came to Positano. We had been dating on and off for near enough six months at this point, but it had always been strictly casual.

For our first date we went for a drink, which turned into oysters and champagne, which turned into wine and cocktails, and chatting until it was much too late for a Wednesday. The following week we went for a long walk where I introduced him to Astrid over brunch and we said goodbye with a swift kiss. The following week we went for dinner and drinks, and in the morning I woke up with him next to me.

'I'm not looking for anything serious,' I said.

'That's fine by me,' he said.

'I'm not even sure I believe in long term love anymore, anyway,' I added.

He shrugged and kissed me on my head.

We carried on like this. Sometimes on, sometimes off, but always, categorically, not a 'thing'. We'd barely speak between dates. I was busy, he was busy and neither of us seemed to have any interest in keeping up a pretense of catching up or small chat. Our time together hung suspended in the moments we were actually with each other. And yet, there was something deeply romantic about the way that, despite it being so resolutely casual, the time we spent together was nourishing. It didn't consist of booty calls or late-night texts, but long meandering conversations, walks in the park, unexpected flowers and implicit respect.

I found him curious. Unlike me, where I have all my cards on the table for the world to see, he, I thought, was reserved. I designed who I imagined him to be in my head and believed that until, slowly but surely, he proved me entirely wrong. I realised he only opened up as and when he decided he wanted to be seen. I had never even considered this to be an option. I have main character energy to a debilitating extent. My efforts to always fill silences, patch over awkward moments and appoint myself as an entertainer in any given situation where the role has not already been filled, felt pointless. I hadn't thought that just being there might be enough.

This only made him more endearing to me, as I recognised that what I had initially thought to be serious comments were subtle little jokes. If I missed them, he never pointed it out, but when I fell into step with his humour I found myself laughing more often than not. He was goofy and silly, relaxed and easy. Being around him didn't make me feel electric sparks or anxious butterflies, but I did feel safe and myself. He didn't care if I was being embarrassing or wearing nipple covers as a top or a little too loud, a little too much, he just accepted that that was who I was. Maybe because neither of us imagined it was going anywhere, we weren't afraid to romance each other. It felt like a safe space to be gentle and kind in a way that was just for the sake of it, without fear of it being misconstrued. He was a self-confessed commitment-phobe and hadn't had a relationship for almost a decade, and I was sworn off them, relishing my singledom, so it seemed like a safe communion.

When my sister asked me if I wanted to bring anyone to her wedding, I thought I might as well ask him and he was more than happy to accompany me as my date. 'I will just sit at the back,' he said. He met my entire extended family within the space of five minutes and took it all in his stride, despite us being a chaotic bunch. I was quick to correct anyone who referred to him as my boyfriend. 'We're just seeing each other,' I'd say to a bemused older relative.

He was so spontaneous it took me by surprise. My fear of relationships had come from a place of starting to see them as an end, an end to freedom and individuality and spontaneity; the beginning of *real* adulting, something I had begun to envision as stuffy and rigid. Only with him, things were more exciting, not less. Everything was carefree, last minute, up to me, 'No worries if not.'

Nine months after our first date, sat in a little Parisian restaurant in Montmartre, I asked J if he thought we should be exclusive.

'I think we should be together, give things a proper go,' came his reply.

I was so stunned that I sat in silence with a garlic-buttered snail dangling off the end of my fork for a full forty-five seconds, which for me is equivalent to forty-five minutes. This wasn't what I had been expecting. All of our conversations thus far on the subject had been about how if there was one thing that was certain, it was that this *wasn't* going to go anywhere. I merely thought exclusivity was a fair step at this point, as it was almost a year in and we were being quite couplely in Paris, and saw each other fairly regularly, so I was more asking if he'd prefer me to stop snogging people every time I went to Archer Street on Northcote Road.

'Are you sure?' I asked, knowing that he really wasn't too certain about relationships and worried he was making a rash decision. I was also worried for myself, because as a serial monogamist I was supposed to be doing exactly the opposite of falling in love with the tall handsome guy that lived round the corner.

'Ok,' I said grinning. 'Let's do it. I love you.'

I don't know if J and I will be together forever, but that doesn't matter. Fuck it, life's short, so why the hell not.

When I said to Francesca that I hated being called an influencer, it was because I can, and always have been able to, see both sides. I genuinely do acknowledge that watching people live ultra-aspirational lives can dim the bright light of your own joy. I still get that inadequacy feeling every now and then. I, too, have scrolled past posts by women whose noses are perfect ski slopes, whose closets make me green with envy, whose relationships look rom-com worthy and who make me feel like I will never be loved like that. But I can rationalise those social media-fuelled insecurities, because I know I have posted content when I have been less than happy, when things have been less than perfect, and that these image-based platforms can only ever give us the tip of the iceberg, the cherry on top, the highlight reel. I get so much from the creators that I follow, but they don't owe me anything in return and, when they no longer serve me, I can just unfollow. I know what these platforms are, how they work and why they work. I do really believe that in order to make social media a more neutral thing, we must take stock of how things make us feel and realise that we don't have to engage and consume all the time.

I wish I could log off more. I have gone on to my friends' Instagrams and felt jealous that their last post was from eight months ago; that they have stories to tell me when I see them that they haven't already shared online; and that no one is making up tall tales about them on gossip websites. I feel embarrassed when I realise maybe one of J's friends knew about my Instagram from before we were together; that when I meet people they may already have a set view of me in their head; that when I say influencer, they think 'terrible person'. Perhaps it's a small price to pay for all the incredible opportunities, but there is power and freedom on both sides.

For most people creating content online, their work is their passion, one that, if successful, they are superfortunate to pursue. But irrespective of intent or impact, the most important thing I have learnt is that followers, validation, expensive clothes or trips abroad will never satiate you as much as laughing so hard with your friends you go from screeching to silent as your vocal cords buckle under the weight of your glee. I have learnt that whilst it can be beautiful to see other couples in love, you will have loves in your life that are singular to you, whether that's with a partner, a parent or a pet, that no one else will ever be able to experience or emulate. And I have learnt that success is actually quite unfulfilling and lonely when it doesn't feel earned, whereas being proud of yourself, knowing you put your all into something, is much more impressive and satisfying than empty accolades.

I now know that no matter how noisy the internet is, how tempting the discourse may be, how many straw-man arguments are wheeled out, you can always just lock your phone, pick up a book, and sit on a park bench with only the sounds of nature and the delight of literature to keep you company. Or you could go dancing until you can't feel your feet, drink enough spicy margaritas to create a lime shortage and snog a stranger or two or three or five. But hey, that's up to you. I don't want to be a bad influence.

ACKNOWLEDGEMENTS

Firstly, thank you so much to the team at Quercus for making my wildest dreams come true. Little bespectacled me is quaking in her boots that I am now an author. Thank you Katy Follain and Nina Sandelson for graciously receiving the pile of words that was my first draft and guiding me gently but firmly to eventually produce this book, of which I am, finally, proud. (Honestly, you should've seen some of the stuff in the first draft – truly terrible.) The process was quite a reckoning for me, but I learnt a lot and I am a much better writer thanks to you both!

Thank you to my agent Francesca Zampi. You got me here, against all odds. No matter how many times I asked if I could just hand the money back, we did it, Joe! Since we first met, you have always had the patience, generosity and kindness to help me believe in my potential, even when I have wanted to give up. What a gift to be able to give. I know everyone who has worked with you past and present feels the same.

Endless, boundless thanks and love to my mum and sisters and dad. I know I didn't let any of you ask me about, let alone read, the book until I had completed it; that I refused to speak about it whatsoever for the year and a bit I was writing it; and that I basically shut down and ignored you whenever the subject was brought up . . . Without you having always been so encouraging of all my singing, acting and creating as a child, I may not have turned out to be as insufferable as I am today and I may never have been able to turn talking about myself into a career. Really, this is all your fault.

To my girls, Poppie Compton, Yas Lewis, Steph Pugh and Izzy Stubbs, you have all been my rocks through many a turbulent relationship, a handful of breakdowns and some very loud snoring over the years. I love you all, forever.

To Grace Campbell, I love you so much, owe you so much and am so glad that our daughters, Eddie and Astrid, are best friends.

To Beth Maitland, sorry I bring you up in everything I have ever done that goes to print. You really should be less inspirational.

To my dearest friends who aren't in the book, I adore you just as much as the ones that are and I will put you in the next one, for balance. Love you, you know who you are. (I will WhatsApp you 'I'm talking about you' to confirm formally and see if you make it this far.)

To J. You were the first person I allowed to read this book apart from my editors, and you, as you always are, were so generous, thoughtful and reassuring. Thank you for correcting me on the difference between Premiership and Premier League rugby. Sorry I said I didn't feel sparks initially. I meant that as a compliment.

To Astrid, thank you for letting me be your mum, I know you can't read, but just know this is the only acknowledgement that I have cried at whilst typing.

And finally, to my followers, thank YOU. None of this would be possible without you. Like, literally.